Pre-Primer – Grade 8

Spanish Reading
INVENTORY

Second Edition

Jerry L. Johns
Northern Illinois University, Emeritus

Mayra C. Daniel
Northern Illinois University

Kendall Hunt
p u b l i s h i n g   c o m p a n y
www.kendallhunt.com/readingresources.html

Book Team

Chairman and Chief Executive Officer   Mark C. Falb
President and Chief Operating Officer   Chad M. Chandlee
Vice President, Higher Education   David L. Tart
Director of Publishing Partnerships   Paul B. Carty
Editorial Manager   Georgia Botsford
Vice President, Operations   Timothy J. Beitzel
Assistant Vice President, Production Services   Christine E. O'Brien
Senior Production Editor   Melissa King
Cover Designer   Jenifer Chapman

Author Information for Professional Development and Workshops

Jerry L. Johns, Ph.D.
Consultant in Reading
E-mail: *jjohns@niu.edu*
Fax: 815-899-3022

Mayra C. Daniel, Ed.D.
Northern Illinois University
Department of Literacy Education
DeKalb, IL 60115
E-mail: *mcdaniel@niu.edu*
Office: 815-753-8379

Ordering Information

Address: Kendall Hunt Publishing Company
              4050 Westmark Drive
              Dubuque, IA 52002
Telephone: 800-247-3458, ext. 4
Website: www.kendallhunt.com
Fax: 800-772-9165

Contents

Section 3. Determining the Student's Three Reading Levels and Instructional Uses   37

PART 2   Spanish Reading Inventory Forms and Performance Booklets   51

Preface

The purpose of the Spanish Reading Inventory is to help teachers and other professionals determine a student's reading proficiency in Spanish. A series of word lists and passages ranging from the early stages of reading (pre-primer) through eighth grade are read by the student. Based on the student's comprehension and word recognition, an estimate is made of his or her reading ability.

A number of passages from the Basic Reading Inventory were used as a basis for Spanish interpretive translations and adaptations.

Acknowledgments

Many individuals assisted with the development and refinement of the Spanish Reading Inventory. In California, a number of teachers and Spanish speakers from different countries read the translations and offered advice: Alicia Holt and Barbara Conley, bilingual teachers at La Joya School in Salinas; Félix Guzmán, Rosario Garza, and Samuel Espitia, bilingual instructional assistants at La Joya School; Felipe Gómez, a grocery clerk and college student from Redwood City, his wife, Claudia Parras, and his brother, Juan Carlos Gómez, a high school student; and Donald Sarria, a businessman from San Jose.

Nancy Carter, bilingual language arts research specialist, reviewed a near-final draft of the materials and suggested names of individuals to help fieldtest or critique the inventory. We also made several contacts. Special thanks are extended to the following individuals for their kind assistance: Miriam Alonso, Chicago, IL; Hans Stiehl, Chicago, IL; Gerardo Herrera, Rockford, IL; Maria Luz Morales Galvan, Michoacán, Mexico; Perla Stefanski, Rockford, IL; Juanita Castro, Rockford, IL; Verna Rentsch, Rockford, IL; Lucrecia de Palomo, Guatemala; Ani Daniel, Chicago, IL; Kathleen Gallagher, Chicago, IL; Leila Lituma, Chicago, IL; Margaret Amaya-Rodríguez, Houston, TX; Judy Brunhober, Santa Ana, CA; Marie F. Doan, Port St. Lucie, FL; Socorro García, Houston, TX; Cristela F. González, Houston, TX; Sandra Gutiérrez, Houston, TX; Donna Hattendorf, Oak Brook, IL; James E. Hitt, Whittier, CA; Rosa K. Iracheta, Eagle Pass, TX; Mary Mosley, Fort Pierce, FL; Carmen Peterson, Ft. Pierce, FL; Mara Puente, Mission, TX; Delia M. Robles, La Feria, TX; Ana Rodriguez, Port St. Lucie, FL; Peggy Sperry, Turlock, CA; Andrea Stanton, DeKalb, IL; Mary Zonta, Carol Stream, IL; Jillian Losee, DeKalb, IL; Christina Mogensen, Sterling, IL; and Connie Ayala, Immokalee, FL.

Finally, several hundred boys and girls read the word lists and passages. Their readings provided valuable input that was incorporated into the final version of the Spanish Reading Inventory.

Jerry & Mayra

About the Authors

Jerry L. Johns has been recognized as a distinguished teacher, writer, outstanding teacher educator, and popular professional development speaker for schools, school districts, and conferences. His more than 700 presentations have involved travel throughout the United States and 12 countries. He has taught students from kindergarten through graduate school and also served as a reading teacher. Professor Johns spent his career at Northern Illinois University. He was also a Visiting Professor at Western Washington University and the University of Victoria in British Columbia.

Professor Johns served in leadership positions at the local, state, national, and international levels. He has been president of the International Reading Association, the Illinois Reading Council, the Association of Literacy Educators and Researchers, and the Northern Illinois Reading Council. He also served on the Board of Directors for each of these organizations as well as the American Reading Forum. In addition, Dr. Johns has served on numerous committees of the International Reading Association and other professional organizations.

Dr. Johns has authored or coauthored nearly 300 articles, monographs, and research studies as well as numerous professional books. His *Basic Reading Inventory*, now in the tenth edition, is widely used in undergraduate and graduate classes as well as by practicing teachers. Among his more than 15 coauthored books to help teachers strengthen their reading instruction are *Teaching Reading Pre-K–Grade 3, Fluency: Differentiated Interventions and Progress-Monitoring Assessments, Comprehension and Vocabulary Strategies for the Elementary Grades,* and *Reading and Learning Strategies: Middle Grades through High School.* Professor Johns currently serves on the editorial advisory boards for *Reading Psychology* and the *Illinois Reading Council Journal.*

Dr. Johns has been the recipient of numerous awards for his contributions to the profession. The Illinois Reading Council honored him with the induction into the Reading Hall of Fame. Other recognitions include the Alpha Delta Literacy Award for Scholarship, Leadership, and Service to Adult Learners and the A.B. Herr Award for outstanding contributions to the field of reading. He also received the Outstanding Teacher Educator in Reading Award presented by the International Reading Association, the Champion for Children Award presented by the HOSTS Corporation, and the Laureate Award from the Association of Literacy Educators and Researchers for life-long contributions to the field of reading.

Mayra C. Daniel is an Associate Professor in the Department of Literacy Education at Northern Illinois University, De Kalb, IL. She began her K–12 teaching career as a Middle School Spanish and English Teacher and later worked with immigrant populations and heritage language speakers. She taught at levels K–12 for fifteen years. She later taught Spanish at the tertiary level for six years. Being Cuban, she and her family were part of the first wave of immigrants who fled Castro's communist regime to the United States in 1961. Because of the lack of bilingual programs in education at the time in Chicago, Illinois, where her family settled, she learned English the hard way—through immersion.

Currently, Dr. Daniel's work with practicing teachers within the continental United States and in Guatemala focuses on preparing educators to plan and modify curriculum so that it appropriately addresses the needs of multilingual, multicultural populations of students. In Guatemala, she works with practicing teachers, teacher educators, and students enrolled in Guatemala's Normal Schools. Her research focuses on preparing teachers to instruct and evaluate learners of a second language or students she affectionately calls bilinguals-in-the-making.

Dr. Daniel is active in the Teachers to Speakers of Other Languages Organization (TESOL) and is the chair-elect of TESOL's Bilingual Interest Section for the 2009–2010 academic year. She has been awarded the Jerry Johns Promising Researcher Award by the Association of Literacy Educators and Researchers. She was inducted into the Phi Beta Delta, Zeta Gamma Chapter Honor Society for International Scholars. She was recognized by the Northern Illinois University College of Education for her Exceptional Contribution to Service and Outreach. In 2009, Dr. Daniel was named National Team Reviewer for the National Council for Accreditation of Teacher Educators. She is a TESOL National Program Reviewer. Dr. Daniel has presented at over 60 state, national, and international presentations. She has authored or coauthored more than 30 articles for professional journals and four books.

PART 1
Spanish Reading Inventory Manual

Overview of the Spanish Reading Inventory

Assessing English Language Learners (ELLs) in Spanish

Throughout the United States (US), students who speak a language other than English are evaluated to establish their English language proficiency before being placed in classrooms. Each year ELLs' progress is evaluated to verify if they are properly placed in educational programs. A problem when evaluation is conducted solely in English is that it gives information about only one aspect of the picture. Evaluations that only look at the student's ability to speak English do not consider or acknowledge the level of literacy the student may have in the home language. You need this information to plan instruction for your Spanish-speaking ELLs. Although many immigrant ELLs have experienced appropriate schooling prior to arrival in the US, not all immigrants begin their education in the US after having attended schools in their country of origin. Some ELLs are recent arrivals while others are heritage language speakers who have grown up interacting with their families either totally or partially in Spanish within the US. Professionally-designed language proficiency tests have long been used to evaluate the language proficiency of ELLs, whether born in the US or abroad. The problem with such evaluations, however, is that they are infrequently administered in both English and Spanish. Not all language proficiency tests are available in Spanish. Even when an ELL is evaluated in Spanish, only a small part of the test will address a student's reading. Therefore, these tests offer few suggestions for curriculum development and modifications.

This Spanish Reading Inventory balances the evaluation process and provides the means to assess an ELL's Spanish literacy and compare it to the results, if desired, to a reading evaluation conducted in English. The Spanish Reading Inventory will give you knowledge of your students' literacy skills in the learner's home/primary language. It will allow you to observe what an ELL does when reading and decide where you need to begin reading instruction with the student. The word lists, reading passages, and questions in this Spanish Reading Inventory facilitate your examination of both a student's miscues and comprehension level. As the examiner, you will have the time to notice, jot down, and later examine specific miscues. This information will help you design classroom instruction and provide differentiated interventions.

Making Instruction and Interventions Responsive to Students

"Effective reading instruction begins with assessment" (Cooter & Perkins, 2007, p. 6). For more than sixty years, the informal reading inventory has been regarded as "the comprehensive assessment instrument of choice" (Walpole & McKenna, 2006, p. 592). With the impact of Reading First (part of the No Child Left Behind legislation) and the recent emphasis on Response to Intervention (RTI), informal assessments like the Spanish Reading Inventory help to identify students who are struggling in reading and serve as the basis for instructional interventions in classrooms, resource rooms, and special education. Fink (2006, p. 131), for example, notes that informal reading inventories "can determine both the level and type of instruction likely to be most beneficial for each student." She also stresses that estimates of each student's three reading levels (independent, instructional, and frustration) are provided to make "planning instruction easier and more effective" (p. 131). If your students are to reach their potential, you must provide responsive instruction. A fundamental principle of responsive instruction is attention to individual differences, and teachers are the critical core in making a difference in reading achievement (International Reading Association, 2007). You can differentiate instructional interventions to help students make significant progress in reading. While methods come and go, teachers are the core in providing quality reading instruction that is responsive to their students. Responsive instruction has many qualities, and a fundamental principle is attention to individual differences.

Students have the right to be evaluated with appropriate reading assessments (Bass, Dasinger, Elish-Piper, Matthews, & Risko, 2008). A position statement of the International Reading Association (2000), titled *Making a Difference Means Making It Different*, notes that students "have a right to reading assessment that identifies their strengths as well as their needs . . ." (p. 7). The Spanish Reading Inventory is one resource to help gather information for instructional decision making in reading. It can be used to estimate the student's instructional level—the level at which the student is challenged but not overwhelmed. It is the level where the student can profit from reading instruction (Spiegel, 1995). If students are placed in instructional materials where they are able to pronounce approximately 95 percent of the words, they tend to be successful readers who are on task (Adams, 1990). Unfortunately, many students are placed in materials that are too difficult for them (Allington, 2009). These students fail to benefit much from lessons using grade-level texts (O'Connor, Bell, Harty, Larkin, Sacker, & Zigmond, 2002).

Responsive instructional interventions are more likely to be provided if teachers can use assessment tools to determine a student's strengths and weaknesses in reading (International Reading Association, 2007; Kibby, 1995). According to Manning (1995), valuable information can be obtained by noting the behaviors of students as they read orally in instructional materials. The Spanish Reading Inventory provides one means through which you can systematically gain insights into a student's reading. You can study and analyze a student's abilities in word identification, fluency, and comprehension. The information gained can be an important basis for responsive instruction and high-quality instructional interventions. Taylor, Pearson, Clark, and Walpole (2002) noted that systematic assessment of student progress figured prominently in their findings of effective schools. "Assessment practices should enrich teaching and learning" (Tierney, 1998, p. 388). The Spanish Reading Inventory can help you "to become better informed and make better decisions" (Tierney, 1998, p. 388). Such decisions can be used to help develop differentiated literacy plans for students (Felknor, 2000). The end result should help students become more efficient and effective readers.

Components of the Spanish Reading Inventory

The Spanish Reading Inventory is an individually administered informal reading test. Composed of a series of graded word lists and graded passages, the inventory will help you gain insights into students' reading behavior. Inventory results will help support the daily instructional decisions you need to make. Five types of comprehension questions follow each passage: topic, fact, inference, evaluation, and vocabulary. This manual explains the purposes of the

Spanish Reading Inventory, gives directions for administering and scoring the inventory, and provides concrete assistance for interpreting the findings of the inventory so that the results can be used to improve students' reading.

There are two forms (A and B) of the Spanish Reading Inventory. The two forms each contain word lists ranging from pre-primer (beginning reading) through grade three and passages ranging from the pre-primer level through the eighth grade. Four numerals are used to code the grade level of the word lists and/or passages in the Spanish Reading Inventory above the primer level. Table 1.1 contains the code.

Table 1.1
Code of Grade Levels for the Two Forms of the Spanish Reading Inventory

Grade Level	Form of the Spanish Reading Inventory	
	A	B
Pre-Primer 1	AAA	BBB
Pre-Primer 2	AA	BB
Primer	A	B
1	A 7141	B 7141
2	A 8224	B 8224
3	A 3183	B 3183
4	A 5414	B 5414
5	A 8595	B 8595
6	A 6867	B 6867
7	A 3717	B 3717
8	A 8183	B 8183

Pre-Primer and Primer Levels

For the pre-primer and primer levels, capital letters designate the level.

- The pre-primer levels are designated by two or three capital letters. For example, AAA refers to pre-primer 1 in Form A; BB refers to pre-primer 2 in Form B.
- The primer level is designated by one capital letter. For example, B refers to the primer level in Form B; A refers to the primer level in Form A.

Grade Levels 1–8

For the remaining levels, you can determine the grade level of the word list or passage by determining which two numerals are identical.

In Table 1.1, for example, A 7141 indicates that the word list or passage in Form A is at the first-grade level because there are two 1's. The code B 8183 indicates the word list or passage in Form B is at the eighth-grade level because there are two 8's. A similar procedure is followed for the remaining word lists and passages.

Purposes of the Spanish Reading Inventory

On the basis of the student's performance on the word lists and graded passages, you can gain insights into the student's:

- **Independent reading level**—The level at which the student reads fluently with excellent comprehension.
- **Instructional reading level**—The level at which the student can make maximum progress in reading with high-quality instruction.

- **Frustration level**—The level at which the student is unable to pronounce many of the words and/or is unable to comprehend the material satisfactorily.
- **Strategies for word identification**—Evaluate the student's sight vocabulary and ability to use phonic analysis, context clues, and structural analysis to pronounce words.
- **Fluency**—Determine the student's rate of reading (in words per minute), assess accuracy in word identification, and make informal judgments about phrasing and expression.
- **Strengths and weaknesses in comprehension**—Evaluate the student's ability to answer various types of comprehension questions.
- **Listening level**—Determine the highest level of material that the student can comprehend when it is read to him or her.

Observations can also be made regarding the student's interests, attitudes, self-monitoring strategies, general approach to various tasks, and reading behavior (such as engagement, persistence, and predictions).

Background Information on Reading Levels and the Listening Level

A major function of the Spanish Reading Inventory is to identify a student's three reading levels: independent, instructional, and frustration. Numerous questions have been raised about standards for evaluating a student's performance on reading inventories (Johns, 1976; 1990). Although some research (Anderson & Joels, 1986; Johns & Magliari, 1989) indicates that the original criteria suggested by Betts (1946) are too high for determining the instructional level for students in the primary grades, other studies (Hays, 1975; Homan & Klesius, 1985; Morris, 1990; Pikulski, 1974) report contradictory findings. In addition, Ekwall (1974, 1976) has presented evidence that supports retaining the traditional Betts criteria. Remember that the numerical criteria for reading levels are not *absolute standards*; they are *guidelines* to help you evaluate a student's reading in conjunction with observational data. Each of the three reading levels presented here will be considered from two viewpoints: the teacher's and the student's. The listening level will also be discussed. Note that each reading level is characterized by both quantitative (numerical) and qualitative (behavioral) data.

CAUTION!

What Is the Independent Reading Level?

Level	Characteristics	Types of Reading
Independent (Easy)	Excellent comprehension (90%+) Excellent word recognition (99%+) Few or no repetitions Very fluent	All schoolwork and reading expected to be done alone Pleasure reading Informational reading

Teacher's Viewpoint—Independent Reading Level

The independent reading level is that level at which the student can read fluently without teacher assistance. In other words, the student can read the materials independently with excellent comprehension. This is the level of supplementary and recreational reading. The material should not cause the student any difficulty. If the student reads orally, the reading should be expressive with accurate attention to punctuation. At this level, the student's reading should be free from finger pointing, vocalizing, lip movement, poor phrasing, and other indications of general tension or problems with the reading material.

In order to be considered at the student's independent level, materials should be read with near-perfect accuracy in terms of word recognition. Even in a situation of oral reading at sight, the student should generally not make more than one significant miscue in each 100 running words. With respect to comprehension, the student's score, when 10 comprehension questions of various types are asked, should be no lower than 90 percent. In short, the student should be able to fully understand the material.

If a retelling strategy is used, a student "will be able to reflect most of the content of a selection and will reflect it in an organized fashion." In a narrative passage, the student will recount events in the proper order. In expository passages, the student's retelling will reflect the text structure or organization of that material. For example, a passage with the main idea followed by supporting details will usually be retold in the same manner (Johnson, Kress, & Pikulski, 1987, p. 14).

It is important that the above criteria for determining a student's independent reading level be applied with careful teacher judgment. The criteria, especially the near-perfect accuracy for word recognition, may have to be a bit more liberal when evaluating a student's reading in the early grades. A third grader might substitute an entire phrase such as *quebró el vidrio* for *rompió el cristal*. An older student could omit modifiers such as *muchos*. Some omissions and insertions do not seriously interfere with fluency and/or a good understanding of the passage. Miscues of this nature should be regarded as acceptable; they are not significant. If you correctly determine the student's independent reading level, the student will experience little difficulty with materials that are written at or below that particular level.

Student's Viewpoint—Independent Reading Level

Because most students have never heard of the various reading levels, they would not refer to the percentages and related behavioral characteristics just described. A student might, however, describe the independent reading level in these terms: "I can read this book by myself, and I understand what I read. I like reading books like this; they're easy."

What Is the Instructional Reading Level?

Level	Characteristics	Types of Reading
Instructional (Just right; comfortable)	Good comprehension (75–85%) Good word recognition (95%+) Fluent A few unknown words Some repetitions	Guided reading Basal instruction Texts used for instruction

Teacher's Viewpoint—Instructional Reading Level

The instructional reading level is that level at which the student can, theoretically, make maximum growth in reading. It is the level at which the student is challenged but not frustrated. Many teachers are interested in finding the student's instructional level so they can provide classroom reading materials at that level (Felknor, Winterscheidt, & Benson, 1999; McTague, 1997). Allington (2009) considers matching students with materials at their instructional levels critical for students who are behind in reading. This is the level of materials used in guided reading groups. At the instructional level, the student should be free from externally observable symptoms of difficulty, such as finger pointing, produced by the reading materials. Although the student might experience some difficulties when reading classroom materials at sight, most of these difficulties should be overcome after the student has had an opportunity to read the same material silently. In other words, oral rereading should be definitely improved over oral reading at sight. If the student is to make maximum progress from instruction, he or she should encounter no more difficulty in reading materials than can be adequately dealt with through high-quality instruction.

In order to be considered at the student's instructional level, materials should be read with no more than 5 miscues in each 100 words in terms of word recognition. According to Adams (1990, p. 113), "there is evidence that achievement in reading is improved by placement in materials that a student can read orally with a low error rate (2 percent to 5 percent), and that students placed in materials that they read with greater than 5 percent errors tend to be off-task during instruction." Additional research by Berliner (1981) and Gambrell, Wilson, and Gantt (1981) also support the 95 percent criterion. In addition, Enz (1989) found that placing students using higher standards resulted in greater engagement, higher success rates, and more positive attitudes toward reading. A more recent study (O'Connor, Bell, Harty, Larkin, Sackor, & Zigmond, 2002) found that students who read materials at their reading (instructional) level made greater gains in fluency compared to students who read grade-level materials. Although some difficulties will probably arise in word recognition, the student should be able to use contextual cues, phonics, and other strategies to decode most unknown words. In terms of comprehension, the student should miss fewer than 3 of 10 comprehension questions.

If a retelling strategy is used, a student responding to instructional level materials will "reflect less content than at an independent level. The organization of the passage will be less complete and some minor misinterpretations and inaccuracies may begin to appear." In essence, the student is able to share the overall sense and content of the passage (Johnson, Kress, & Pikulski, 1987, p. 17).

It is at the instructional level that the student will have the best opportunity to build new reading strategies. This is the level at which guided reading instruction is likely to be most successful (Lenski, 1998). Teachers need to be sure that books used for reading instruction are at students' instructional levels.

Student's Viewpoint—Instructional Reading Level

A student might describe the instructional level in these terms: "I can understand what I am taught from this reading book. Some of the words are hard to understand, but after the teacher gives me some help, the story is easy to read."

What Is the Frustration Level?

Level	Characteristics	Types of Reading
Frustration (Too hard)	Weak comprehension (≤50%) Weak word recognition (≤90%) Word-by-word reading Many unknown words Rate is likely to be slow Lack of expression Fluency lacking Fidgeting	Occasional self-selected material when interest and background knowledge are high Materials for diagnostic purposes Avoid instructional materials at this level

Teacher's Viewpoint—Frustration Level

The frustration level is that level at which the student should not be given materials to read. A serious problem in many classrooms is that a large number of students are asked to read books at their frustration levels. Students at their frustration levels are unable to deal effectively with the reading material. Numerous behavioral characteristics may be observed if students are attempting to read materials that are too difficult for them. Some students may actually refuse to continue reading their books. Other students may exhibit lack of expression in oral reading, lip movement during silent reading, difficulty in pronouncing words, word-by-word reading, and/or finger pointing. A study by Jorgenson (1977) found that as reading material became more difficult, teachers judged their students as becoming more impatient, disturbing to the classroom, and reliant on persons other than themselves for directions.

The criteria for the frustration level, in addition to the behavioral characteristics just noted, are 10 or more miscues in every 100 words (90 percent or less) and comprehension scores of 50 percent or less. For example, a student who could not correctly pronounce 90 or more words in a 100-word selection and who could not answer at least half of the questions asked by the teacher is likely trying to read material that is too difficult.

If a retelling strategy is used, "materials at a frustration level are recalled incompletely or in a rather haphazard fashion. Bits of information may be recalled, but they are not related in any logical or sequential order." Questions asked by the teacher tend to go unanswered. In addition, behaviors such as finger pointing and tenseness may appear (Johnson, Kress, & Pikulski, 1987, p. 20).

Student's Viewpoint—Frustration Level

Because reading materials at this level are too difficult for the student, it is likely that the frustration level would be described in these terms: "This book is too hard. I hate to read when books are this hard. I'm lost." Other students will say nothing when books are too difficult for them to read, but the perceptive teacher will note when books are at a student's frustration level. The teacher can then provide or suggest other materials that are at the student's independent or instructional levels.

What Is the Listening Level?

The listening level is the *highest* level at which the student can understand material that is read *to* him or her. Determining this level can help you ascertain whether a student has the potential to improve as a reader. When a substantial difference exists between the student's instructional level and listening level (generally a year or more), it usually indicates that the student should be able to make significant growth in reading achievement with appropriate instruction. The larger the difference, the more reason to believe that the student can profit from instruction that is responsive to his or her needs in reading. Many students who struggle with reading can improve if they are given high-quality instruction, placed in reading materials at their instructional levels, and have their progress monitored regularly.

The criterion for the listening level is a minimum comprehension score of at least 70 percent. In other words, the student should miss no more than 3 of 10 comprehension questions. It is also important for you to informally assess whether the student's vocabulary and language structure in conversations are as complex as that used in the reading passage.

Schell (1982), after reviewing several studies relating to the listening level, warned against **CAUTION!** using the procedure with students in grades one through three. He argued that reading comprehension and listening comprehension are not the same for students in the primary grades; moreover, neither grow at approximately equal rates until about sixth grade. For these reasons, you should not use the listening level procedure with students in the primary grades.

Preparation for Assessment

Understand the Procedures

The person who administers this assessment must be biliterate Spanish-English. To prepare for assessment, you need to be familiar with the procedures for administering and scoring the Spanish Reading Inventory. These procedures are detailed in Section 2. What is needed for assessment? There are five basic items:

1. This manual or the summary of administration and scoring procedures on page 35.
2. The student copies of the word lists and passages in this manual.
3. A piece of heavy paper to cover a word list or passage when necessary.
4. A performance booklet in which you will record the student's responses. These booklets are in this manual and may be reproduced for noncommercial educational purposes.
5. A desk or table and two chairs. It is recommended that right-handed teachers seat the student on their left. Left-handed teachers should do the opposite.

Overview of Administration and Scoring Procedures

To determine a student's reading proficiency, it is recommended that you administer the reading tests included in the Spanish Reading Inventory in the manner described below.

Word Recognition in Isolation

Select a graded word list at a reading level that will be easy for the student. Ask the student to pronounce the words at a comfortable rate. Record the student's responses in the sight column beside the corresponding word in the performance booklet.

Return to mispronounced or unknown words for a second attempt and note the student's responses in the analysis column. Administer successive word lists until the student is no longer able to achieve a total of at least 14 words correct or until the student becomes frustrated. Examples of student and teacher copies of word lists are shown in Figure 1-1 on page 11. The actual copies used with the student can be found on pages 54–56.

Scoring Word Recognition in Isolation

Total the correct responses in the sight and analysis columns. Consult the criteria in the scoring guide at the bottom of the teacher's word lists to determine a rough estimate of the reading level achieved on each graded word list.

Word Recognition in Context (Passages)

Ask the student to read aloud the graded passage two levels below the highest independent level achieved on the graded word lists. As the student reads the passage, record miscues on the corresponding copy of the passage found in the performance booklet. A miscue occurs when the student's oral reading of a passage differs from the printed passage. For example, a miscue results if the student says *los* when the word in the passage is *sol*. Substituting *los* for *sol* is called a miscue. Other major types of miscues are omissions, insertions, and mispronunciations. Examples of student and teacher materials are shown in Figure 1-2 on page 12.

List AA		List A	
1. mi		1. abeja	
2. papá		2. juego	
3. sapo		3. silla	
4. no		4. corre	
5. él		5. hizo	
6. vete		6. café	
7. bebé		7. chivo	
8. toma		8. lluvia	
9. luna		9. queso	
10. bonito		10. conejo	
11. pelo		11. helado	
12. todo		12. sobre	
13. ala		13. encima	
14. saluda		14. tenía	
15. va		15. zapato	
16. nido		16. cereza	
17. amigo		17. ciudad	
18. en		18. ayuda	
19. rana		19. dueño	
20. fue		20. guitarra	

54   Form A • Graded Word Lists • Student Copy

Form A • Graded Word Lists • Performance Booklet • Student Copy is on page 54.

List AA (Pre-Primer)	Sight	Analysis	List A (Primer)	Sight	Analysis
1. mi			1. abeja		
2. papá			2. juego		
3. sapo			3. silla		
4. no			4. corre		
5. él			5. hizo		
6. vete			6. café		
7. bebé			7. chivo		
8. toma			8. lluvia		
9. luna			9. queso		
10. bonito			10. conejo		
11. pelo			11. helado		
12. todo			12. sobre		
13. ala			13. encima		
14. saluda			14. tenía		
15. va			15. zapato		
16. nido			16. cereza		
17. amigo			17. ciudad		
18. en			18. ayuda		
19. rana			19. dueño		
20. fue			20. guitarra		
Number Correct			Number Correct		
Total			Total		

Scoring Guide for Graded Word Lists			
Independent	Instructional	Inst./Frust.	Frustration
20 19	18 17 16	15 14	13 or less

Figure 1-1 (Left) Sample Student Copy of Graded Word Lists; (Right) Sample Teacher Copy of Graded Word Lists from Performance Booklet

Scoring Word Recognition in Context (Passages)

To find the word recognition in context score, count the number of miscues (total or significant) in each graded passage and record the numeral in the appropriate box (total or significant). To determine reading levels, consult the appropriate set of criteria in the scoring guide at the bottom of the teacher's passage in the performance booklet. Watch for behaviors associated with frustration: lack of expression, syllable-by-syllable reading, excessive fidgeting, and so on. Discontinue the assessment when frustration is evident.

Comprehension Questions

Ask the comprehension questions in the performance booklet that accompany the passage and record the student's responses. Continue administering graded passages until the student is unable to answer half of the comprehension questions or reads so slowly that a frustration level is apparent.

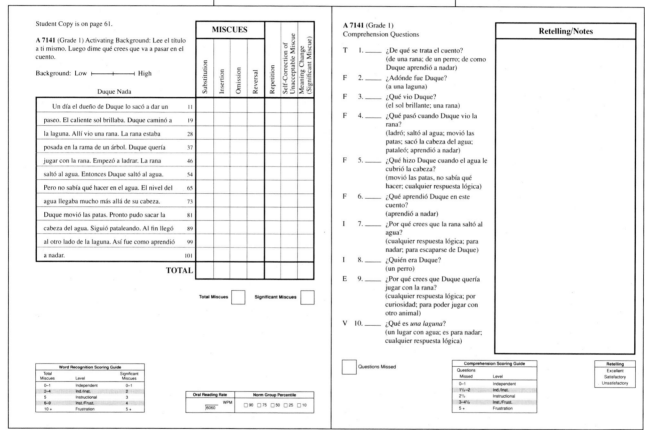

Figure 1-2 (Top) Sample Student Copy of Graded Passage; (Left) Sample Teacher Copy of Graded Passage from Performance Booklet; and (Right) Comprehension Questions from Performance Booklet

Scoring the Comprehension Questions

To find the student's comprehension score for each passage, count the number of comprehension questions answered incorrectly. Then record the numeral in the box below the questions in the performance booklet. To convert the comprehension scores into reading levels, consult the criteria on the scoring guide at the bottom of the teacher's copy in the performance booklet.

Judgment must be exercised at the pre-primer levels because the limited number of questions may not permit precise measurement of achievement. At this level, a retelling of the passage by the student instead of the comprehension questions may be a better indicator of the student's reading ability.

How to Use This Manual

Educators who have limited knowledge of reading inventories will profit by reading this entire manual carefully. It is written to permit self-study. Those who are already familiar with reading inventories, especially the *Basic Reading Inventory* (Johns, 2008), can read sections of interest and use the remainder of the manual as needed.

Administration and Scoring Procedures

The Spanish Reading Inventory is an informal test, and there are no procedures that must be followed rigidly. You must, however, be thoroughly familiar with the recommended procedures for administration prior to asking a student to read the graded word lists and graded passages. Note that the reading inventory will take more time to administer initially until greater familiarity with the procedures is achieved. Facility improves greatly after five or six administrations.

Begin the assessment where the student is likely to find the material easy. The procedure for actually administering and scoring the reading inventory is divided into seven major steps that comprise the subsections of this section.

Establishing Rapport and Gaining Some Insights

If the reading inventory is to yield useful results, it is necessary to obtain the student's cooperation. In an effort to establish rapport, you may wish to give the student some idea about how his or her reading will be evaluated. You may also want to explore the student's interests and answer questions about the assessment procedure. This may help to reduce the anxiety that often accompanies an assessment situation. Note that rapport is not always fully established before the administration of the reading inventory actually begins. In some cases, rapport is steadily increased throughout the assessment. In other cases, interaction between you and the student may become strained during the assessment. If this occurs, take steps to reestablish rapport.

During the early stages of establishing rapport, as well as throughout the administration of the reading inventory, you have the opportunity to gain valuable diagnostic information in several areas. You can appraise the student's oral language facility and background knowledge through informal conversation and observe how well the student responds to specific comprehension questions that are asked after the graded passages are read. You may also ask specific questions such as, "¿Qué haces cuando lees para entender?" to gain insight into how the student views the reading process. When you feel that adequate rapport has been established, it is generally advisable to begin the reading inventory with the graded word lists. Once students have learned to decode in Spanish, they should perform very well on the graded word lists.

Some students, especially young ones or poorer readers, may become tired during the administration of the inventory. In such instances, breaks can be used or the assessment can be spread over two periods. For example, the graded word lists can be given during one sitting and the graded passages can be given at another sitting. Because the graded word lists and passages increase in difficulty, it is a good idea to explain this fact to the student before assessment begins. You might want to encourage students to say "pass," "skip it," "not yet," or "I don't know" when difficult words or questions are encountered.

Administering, Scoring, and Determining Reading Levels from the Graded Word Lists

There are three purposes for giving the graded word lists. First, the word lists will provide the approximate level at which the student should begin reading the graded passages. Second, you will be able to study some of the student's word identification strategies and informally classify the student's word recognition ability as above, at, or below grade level. Third, the word lists can be used to assess the extent of the student's sight vocabulary and knowledge of high-frequency words.

Because the word lists are not a natural reading situation, the best judgments about the student's word identification strategies result from a careful analysis of the student's oral reading of the graded passages. The graded word lists do not assess the student's ability to comprehend and are, therefore, an inappropriate measure of overall reading ability. Students who learn to decode in Spanish will often perform better on the graded word lists than on the comprehension questions following the graded passages.

Administering the Graded Word Lists

To administer the graded word lists, you will need the word lists for the student and the performance booklet in which you will note the student's responses. The recommended procedure for administering the graded word lists is to present the student with the graded list of words and ask him or her to pronounce them at a comfortable rate. If a student reads a word correctly within one second, it is defined as a sight word (Leslie & Caldwell, 1995). As the student reads down each list of words, record the student's responses in a performance booklet. The word list initially selected should, if at all possible, be very easy for the student.

Do not accept a series of separate syllables as a correct word but ask the student to say rapidly what he or she means. All too often, beginning readers may not have made the connection between the syllables and the word and will say the wrong word if asked to do so rapidly. For example, the student may say correctly the separate syllables of the word *saluda: sa- lu- da* on list AA, but may come up with a different word altogether when asked what word he or she said. Use marks over the words on the teacher copy to indicate slow syllable reading (e.g., *sálúdá*). If the correct word is said after such sounding out, give credit in the *analysis* column rather than in the *sight* column.

It is important for you to record the student's responses promptly because any delays are likely to result in incorrect reporting. The use of a tape recorder or digital voice recorder may prove quite helpful for the administrations. The graded word lists are continued until the student is no longer able to achieve a total score of at least 14 correct words or when you observe that the task has become frustrating for the student. Be cognizant that you may hear differences in pronunciation due to the Spanish speaker's country of origin. Do not count dialect miscues against the student. Your judgment plays an important role in the administration of the entire inventory.

Scoring the Graded Word Lists

Three scores (sight, analysis, total) are derived for each graded word list administered to the student (see Figure 2-1). One score represents the student's immediate responses to the words and is called the *sight* score. The second score represents the student's correction of the words missed during the sight presentation. The opportunity for the student to study each word missed in an attempt to pronounce it is called the *analysis* score. If the student does not know or mispronounces any words on the first attempt (that is, at sight), return to each of these words after the student has finished the list and provide the student with an opportunity to analyze the word

List AA (Pre-Primer)	Sight	Analysis	List A (Primer)	Sight	Analysis
1. mi			1. abeja		
2. papá			2. juego		
3. sapo	*sopa*	+	3. silla		
4. no			4. corre		
5. él	*le*	+	5. hizo		
6. vete			6. café		
7. nene			7. chivo		
8. toma			8. lluvia		
9. luna			9. queso		
10. bonito			10. conejo		
11. pelo	*palo*	*palo*	11. helado	*hielo*	*hielo*
12. todo			12. sobre		
13. ala			13. encima		
14. saluda			14. tenía		
15. va			15. zapato	*zapodo*	+
16. nido			16. cereza	*ceraza*	*cereza*
17. amigo			17. ciudad		
18. en			18. ayuda	*ayrída*	*ayrída*
19. rana			19. dueño		
20. fue	*fuí*	+	20. guitarra		
Number Correct	16	3	Number Correct	16	1
Total	19		Total	17	

Scoring Guide for Graded Word Lists			
Independent	Instructional	Inst./Frust.	Frustration
20 19	18 17 16	15 14	13 or less

Figure 2-1 Felipe's Performance on Two Graded Word Lists

in an attempt to arrive at its correct pronunciation. The student's *immediate* responses are recorded in the sight column. The responses the student makes when given an opportunity to study the words missed are recorded in the analysis column. The third score is the total of the sight and analysis scores.

An Example of Scoring the Graded Word Lists

To show how the graded word lists are scored, Figure 2-1 on page 17 contains Felipe's performance on the pre-primer and primer word lists. An empty space next to a word means that Felipe pronounced it correctly. Miscues in word recognition are noted as follows: "DK" means "I don't know." Single letters or phonetic symbols represent Felipe's attempt to pronounce the word. The plus (+) indicates that he corrected a miscalled word. When Felipe said a word which was different from the stimulus word, it is noted in the appropriate column. Other pertinent comments that might have diagnostic significance (for example, reads syllable by syllable; sometimes guesses; quite persistent; gives up easily) can also be noted in the margins of your copy.

Felipe's scores are shown at the bottom of each column of words. For the pre-primer (AA) word list, the score of 16 indicates that he correctly pronounced 16 of the 20 words on the sight presentation. The 4 words not correctly pronounced during the sight presentation were numbers 3, 5, 11, and 20. From his score on the *analysis* column, you can note that Felipe corrected 3 of his initial miscues (numbers 3, 5, and 20), thereby achieving a total score of 19 correct words. At the primer level Felipe achieved a score of 16 on the sight presentation and a total score of 17 because he corrected his initial miscue for number 15.

Use the total number of words Felipe correctly pronounced on each graded word list for a very general idea of his reading. To convert total scores, compare the total number of correct words for each list of words to the scoring guide at the bottom of the word lists in the performance booklet. This scoring guide is also reproduced in Table 2.1.

Table 2.1
Scoring Guide for Graded Word Lists

Independent	Instructional	Inst./Frust.	Frustration
20 19	18 17 16	15 14	13 or less

From Felipe's responses in Figure 2-1, you can note that he achieved a total score of 19 correct words on the pre-primer list. According to the scoring guide below the word lists, a score of 19 would indicate an independent level. The total score of 17 for the primer word list indicates an instructional level. From the results reported thus far, it is not possible to estimate Felipe's frustration level. You would need to continue with additional word lists until Felipe mispronounced 7 words or appeared to be having considerable difficulty. When this point is reached, proceed to the graded passages. Keep in mind that levels estimated with word lists are not valid indications of reading ability because word recognition, not meaning, is being assessed. Recognize the limitations of graded word lists and use this knowledge when scoring and interpreting inventory results.

Recording Word Recognition Scores for the Word Lists

Figure 2-1 shows that Felipe achieved a total score of 19 on the pre-primer list and 17 on the primer list. These scores should then be entered on the summary sheet similar to that shown in Figure 2-2 and reproduced at the beginning of the performance booklets for Forms A and B. To determine the reading levels corresponding to these two scores, consult Table 2.1 or the scoring guide at the bottom of the word lists. Using the criteria, Felipe achieved an independent level

Grade	Word Recognition						Comprehension		Reading Rate	
	Isolation (Word Lists)				Context (Passages)		Oral Reading Form A			
	Sight	Analysis	Total	Level	Miscues*	Level	Questions Missed	Level	Words per Minute (WPM)	Norm Group Percentile
PP2	16	3	19	*Ind.*	0	*Ind.*	0			
P	16	1	17	*Inst.*	1		½			
1	16	1	17		2		0			
2	14	2	16		5		1½			
3	10	2	12		12		5			

*Refers to *total* miscues in this example

Figure 2-2 Summary Sheet for Felipe's Performance on the Spanish Reading Inventory

on the pre-primer word list and an instructional level on the primer word list. Note that the abbreviations *Ind.* and *Inst.* are written on the summary sheet to indicate the levels achieved.

Check your understanding of this procedure by finding the reading levels that correspond to Felipe's scores on the remaining word lists noted in Figure 2-2. This task can be accomplished by taking the total score given in Figure 2-2 for the first-grade word list (17) and finding the corresponding reading level from the scoring guide (Table 2.1). The reading level should then be entered next to the number of words correct. The same procedure can be repeated for the score on the second-grade and third-grade word lists.

Administering, Scoring, and Determining Reading Levels from the Graded Passages

Prior to actually administering the graded passages, you need some system for recording the student's miscues. A miscue is "an oral reading response that differs from the expected response to the written text" (Harris & Hodges, 1981, p. 199). Miscues can "provide a rich source of information for analyzing language and reading development" (Harris & Hodges, 1995, p. 155). Figure 2-3 on page 20 contains examples of miscues and a suggested method for recording them during oral reading. Carefully study and learn or adapt the suggested procedure so that it can be used and referred to later when actual examples of a student's oral reading are considered.

It is important to recognize that all ELLs whose first language is Spanish may make different miscues due to interlanguage influences. Students' prior schooling and the languages that they have been exposed to affect the ways they learn to read in both Spanish and English. Heritage speakers of Spanish may make transfer errors as they generalize features of the environmental print they have seen and tried to read in English as well as the oral and aural language they have mastered in Spanish. Young readers of Spanish do not instinctively know where to place accents. Learning where to place accents is a skill that requires direct instruction. It is difficult for Spanish readers to know where to place accents because they denote that a word does not follow the usual rules of the language in pronunciation. ELLs born in the US have an even more difficult time mastering the rules governing accents. Perhaps it is because they see that English has no accents and assume Spanish is similar. When they attempt to read accented words, the accents confuse them and they often produce miscues that may or may not suggest good progress or grade-level reading development.

A common transfer error that heritage speakers who have been exposed to English make is to voice the sound of the /h/. In Spanish the /h/ is always silent, regardless of its position in a

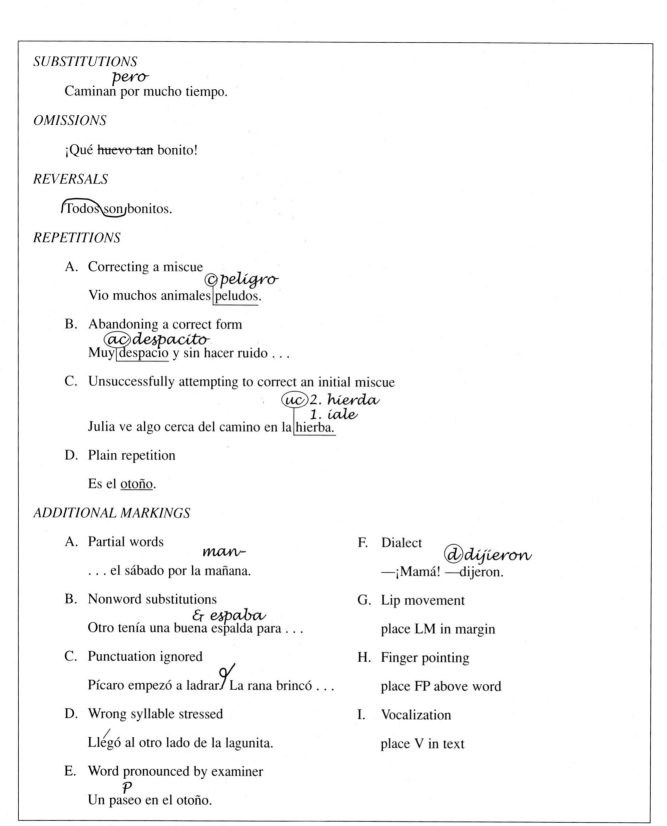

SUBSTITUTIONS

         pero
Caminan por mucho tiempo.

OMISSIONS

    ¡Qué ~~huevo tan~~ bonito!

REVERSALS

    Todos son bonitos.

REPETITIONS

    A. Correcting a miscue

                ©*peligro*
      Vio muchos animales peludos.

    B. Abandoning a correct form

            (ac)despacito
      Muy despacio y sin hacer ruido . . .

    C. Unsuccessfully attempting to correct an initial miscue

                        (uc)2. hierda
                            1. iale
      Julia ve algo cerca del camino en la hierba.

    D. Plain repetition

      Es el <u>otoño</u>.

ADDITIONAL MARKINGS

    A. Partial words

                man-
      . . . el sábado por la mañana.

    B. Nonword substitutions

              & espaba
      Otro tenía una buena espalda para . . .

    C. Punctuation ignored

      Pícaro empezó a ladrar./ La rana brincó . . .

    D. Wrong syllable stressed

      Llégó al otro lado de la lagunita.

    E. Word pronounced by examiner

        P
      Un paseo en el otoño.

    F. Dialect

               (d)dijeron
      —¡Mamá! —dijeron.

    G. Lip movement

      place LM in margin

    H. Finger pointing

      place FP above word

    I. Vocalization

      place V in text

Figure 2-3 A Suggested Method for Recording a Student's Oral Reading Miscues

word. The /j/ and /g/ are two other letters that may complicate reading in Spanish because the sound of these letters depends on the letter which follows. For example, the Spanish words *jinete* and *girasol* both begin with the sound of the /h/ in English yet the word *gato* does not and has a beginning sound akin to that in the word *go*. An interesting phenomenon is the use of the /k/ in Spanish where in the past the /c/ was used. In the US one might see the name *Kristina* rather than *Cristina* which is the standard spelling of this name. Heritage speakers of Spanish might evidence interlanguage interference when writing the word *keso* for *queso*. They are often unable to read the correct spelling of the word until they receive focused instruction. For these reasons it is crucial that bilingual teachers who use this inventory interpret student miscues accurately and with caution in order to use the inventory as the informal assessment it is intended to be.

It is recommended that you begin administering the graded passages at least two levels below the student's highest independent level on the graded word lists. If a student, for example, achieved independent levels on the word lists for the pre-primer, primer, first-, and second-grade levels, it is recommended that you begin the graded passages at the primer level. If the student is unable to read the primer passage at the independent level, go to the next lower level and continue to move down until an independent level is found or the first pre-primer passage is reached. Then, return to the starting point and proceed until the student reaches a frustration level.

TIP

Procedure for Administering the Graded Passages

Before actual reading begins, cover the passage with a heavy sheet of paper so that only the title shows (or the illustration and title for the pre-primer passages). Have the student read the title of the passage silently and predict or share what it might be about. The student's sharing can yield several valuable pieces of information: (1) the background experiences/knowledge the student associates with the title; (2) the student's ability to make predictions; and (3) the student's vocabulary and ability to express himself or herself. During this prereading sharing, you may note the student's ideas and informally evaluate the student's background on a scale of low to high. Place an x on the scale to reflect the level of background knowledge. This scale accompanies each graded passage in the performance booklet and can be found near the top of the page on the left.

Background: Low ├─────────┼─────────┤ High

Do not describe what the passage is about, explain key concepts, or use vocabulary from the passage because the student's comprehension may be artificially enhanced. Once the student has shared or predicted, uncover the passage. The student should then be given a reason to read the passage; for example, to find out more about the title, to check predictions made about the passage, or the like. The student should also be told that comprehension questions will be asked after the passage has been read. Say something like the following, "Read the passage aloud and think about what you're reading. I'll ask you some questions when you're done reading. You won't be able to look back."

CAUTION!

Recording Miscues During Oral Reading and Timing the Reading

While the student is reading from the graded passage, use a performance booklet to keep a careful record of the exact way in which the student reads the passage. Some students may need to be told a word if they pause for ten or fifteen seconds; however, the recommended procedure is to encourage students to read the graded passages using their strategies for word identification without any teacher assistance. The suggested method for recording a student's oral reading, presented in Figure 2-3, should be a valuable aid if you have not yet developed a system for noting miscues. Your major task is to record the manner in which the student reads the passage by noting omissions, insertions, substitutions, and other miscues. In addition, note hesitations, word-by-word reading, finger pointing, monitoring strategies, and so on. If desired, time the student's reading using a timer, a stopwatch, or a watch with a second hand. There is a place in the performance booklet to note the number of seconds it takes the student to read the passage. Performing division will result in the student's rate of reading in words per minute (WPM). Any timing should be done in an inconspicuous manner because some students, if they see they are being timed, will probably not read in their usual way. In addition, some students may focus more on pronouncing words quickly than trying to understand the passage (Johns, 2007). Further discussion of how to determine rate of reading is found under Rate of Reading on page 30 later in this section.

Three Ways to Assess Comprehension

After the student finishes reading the passage, assess comprehension by asking the comprehension questions, using retelling, or combining retelling with the questions. Initially, you may prefer to ask the comprehension questions, at least in the first several administrations of the reading inventory.

1. **Ask Comprehension Questions.** Each reading passage above the pre-primer levels contains 10 comprehension questions. The general procedure is to remove or cover the passage and ask the student the comprehension questions. Write the student's verbatim responses to the comprehension questions or underline the "answers" given in the performance booklets. Noting the student's responses will make scoring the questions much easier. You will also be able to analyze the reasoning used by the student. **The student's answers to the comprehension questions need not conform exactly to the answers in the performance booklets**; responses similar in meaning to the printed answer should be scored as correct. In addition, some students may need to be told that the answers to some questions (vocabulary, evaluation, and inference) are not stated directly in the passage. For these questions, always give credit for responses that demonstrate understanding and/or logical thinking. **Answers in parentheses that are separated by semicolons mean that only one of the answers must be given for full credit (unless indicated otherwise).**

Do not help the student arrive at the correct answers to the questions (use a + for questions answered correctly). If a comprehension question is answered incorrectly (use a −), note the student's response and go on to the next question. You may, however, ask for clarification if the answer for a particular question is not clear. Neutral probes such as "Tell me more," "What else?" or "Explain that further" often help students elaborate on partial answers. Half credit (use ½) may be given for partial answers. Continue with subsequent passages until the student is unable to answer satisfactorily at least half of the comprehension questions or makes many miscues.

2. **Use Retelling.** Retelling is sometimes referred to as free recalls plus probes (questions or imperative statements). McCormick (2003, p. 158) notes several advantages to using retellings or free recalls plus probes. They can assist in "determining whether students have noted important information, whether they can reproduce it in a manner that makes sense, and whether their background knowledge has an effect on the way they interpret the substance of the text." You can also informally assess the student's short-term retention. In retelling, the student is asked to orally recall a passage after it has been read. You could say, "After you have read the passage, you will be asked to retell it in your own words."

Other ways to initiate the retelling include the following probes:

- Tell me what the passage (story or text) is about.
- Tell me as much as you can about what you have just read.
- What is the passage (story or text) about?

TIP

Goodman, Watson, and Burke (2005) have offered suggestions for gaining proficiency in using a retelling strategy to assess a student's comprehension. A few of their suggestions for the use of retelling procedures include:

- familiarity with the passage,
- not giving the student information from the passage,
- asking open-ended questions, and
- retaining any nonwords or name changes given by the student.

Once you become familiar with the graded passages in the Spanish Reading Inventory, it is possible to use a retelling strategy to assess comprehension. First, invite the student to tell everything about the passage that has just been read. Then ask specific questions without giving the student information that has not already been mentioned. Through experience, you can gain confidence in extracting the main ideas and important details in the passages without asking the comprehension questions.

There are some probes that teachers have found useful. Consider adapting and using the following probes (Lipson & Wixson, 2003, p. 283):

- Tell me that story.
- Tell me more about what you have read.
- Tell me more about what happened.
- Tell me more about the people you just read about.
- Tell me more about where this happened.

Lipson and Wixson (2003, pp. 283–284) have also suggested different prompts for narrative and informational text. Because Form A contains narrative passages, and Form B contains informational selections, some sample prompts for the two major types of text are provided below for your use.

Eliciting Narrative Retellings (Form A contains narrative passages)
- How is the setting in the story important?
- What happens to get the story started?
- What is the main problem the characters face?
- How do the characters solve the main problem?

Eliciting Expository (Informational) Retellings (Form B contains informational selections)
- What is the big idea in this selection?
- Why do you think the author wrote this piece?
- How does the author organize the information to share the major ideas?
- What are the main ideas and important details?

To judge student retelling, the categories *excellent* (independent level), *satisfactory* (instructional level), and *unsatisfactory* (frustration level) may be used. At the independent level, the student recalls central or key events, remembers important facts, retains the sequence of events, and relates most of the content in an organized manner. At the instructional level, the student recalls most central or key events, remembers *some* important facts, retains the *general* sequence of events, and relates an overall sense of the content. At the frustration level, the student typically recalls bits of information in a rather haphazard manner with little apparent organization. There is ample space for retelling notes beside the comprehension questions in the performance booklet. If you choose to use retelling, circle excellent, satisfactory, or unsatisfactory in the retelling box at the bottom of the space for retelling notes in the performance booklet.

While retelling is a viable option, it "is not an easy procedure for students, no matter what their ages" (Morrow, 1988, p. 128). In addition, retelling requires considerable teacher judgment, and there is no widely used, generally accepted criteria for judging student retellings of passages. Harris and Sipay (1990) also note that retellings place a heavy demand on the student's ability to retrieve and organize information in the passage. Johnson, Kress, and Pikulski (1987) believe that it is somewhat premature to recommend retelling for widespread practical use.

3. **Combine Retelling with the Questions.** In actual practice, you may feel more comfortable in combining the retelling strategy with some of the comprehension questions. This procedure permits you to maintain the necessary flexibility to gather the information needed to make an accurate assessment of the student's understanding of the passage. The recommended procedure is to invite retelling and put an asterisk or R (for retelling) beside the comprehension questions answered. The remaining questions can be asked after the retelling. This technique capitalizes on the strengths of both assessment procedures while minimizing their weaknesses.

Scoring Felipe's Graded Passage

Figure 2-4 on page 25 contains Felipe's oral reading performance on a second-grade passage. The notations indicate that he substituted *explotar* for *explorar, ellas* for *huellas, cercaba* for *acercaba*, and *corría* for *vieron*. These four substitutions were not corrected. He also omitted *robles*. Based on a total (quantitative) count, Felipe made 5 miscues. The numeral 5 is recorded in the "Total Miscues" box to the bottom right of the passage.

On the 10 comprehension questions in Figure 2-5, Felipe responded freely and demonstrated the ability to answer various types of questions. (A + indicates correct responses; a – indicates incorrect responses; ½ indicates half credit; underlining indicates student's responses.) Felipe missed 1½ questions, but his understanding of the passage was quite good. From the general criteria for the three reading levels at the bottom of Figure 2-4, it would appear that this passage is at Felipe's instructional level, because he made 5 *total* miscues and had comprehension in the *Ind./Inst.* range as indicated in the scoring guide in Figure 2-5.

In counting total miscues, a number of special considerations are warranted. They are noted below. It is important that all this information be considered carefully when analyzing the student's word identification and comprehension.

- Self-corrections provide evidence that the student is monitoring his or her reading, and you may prefer not to count such miscues. Numerous self-corrections, however, impact fluency and rate of reading. If such miscues are not counted, they should still be considered as a qualitative source of information in the overall determination of the student's reading levels.

- Dialect variations, hesitations, and repetitions should not be included in the count of total miscues although they may be recorded for later study and analysis. Hesitations and repetitions impact fluency and may offer clues to helpful instructional interventions.

- The *consistent* mispronunciation of a word more than once in a passage should only be counted once. For example, if a student reads *Christina* for *Catalina* repeatedly in the passage, it should be counted as only one miscue. This same guideline also applies to situations where a particular word is used for a proper name or any other word.

- If a student omits an entire line, it should be counted as one miscue. Such an omission may impact the student's ability to answer one or more of the comprehension questions.

Student Copy is on page 62.

A 8224 (Grade 2) Activating Background: Lee el título a ti mismo. Luego dime qué crees que va a pasar en el cuento.

Background: Low ├────X────┤ High

Jorge está en las Montañas

MISCUES							
	Substitution	Insertion	Omission	Reversal	Repetition	Self-Correction of Unacceptable Miscue	Meaning Change (Significant Miscue)
Era la primera vez que Jorge iba camping con — 9							
su familia. ¡Estaba tan contento de estar en las — 18							
montañas! En cuanto prepararon la casa de — 25							
campaña, él y su papá empezaron a _explotar_ ~~explorar~~ el — 34	1						1
área. Encontraron ~~robles~~ grandes, pinos — 39		1					.5
gigantes, y muchas clases de flores. — 45							
De pronto notaron unas pequeñas huellas _ellas_ que — 52	1						1
parecían ser de animales. Vieron un ratón que — 60							
se _cercaba_ acercaba a un árbol y se metía en un pequeño — 71	1						
agujero de éste. El ratón fue el único animal que — 81							
corría vieron. Jorge sentía curiosidad por saber si todas — 89	1						.5
las huellas eran las del ratoncito. Lo último que — 98							
Jorge vio fue el nido de un pájaro en lo alto de — 110							
un árbol. — 112							
TOTAL	4	0	1	0			3

Total Miscues [5]   Significant Miscues [3]

Word Recognition Scoring Guide		
Total Miscues	Level	Significant Miscues
0–1	Independent	0–1
2–4	Ind./Inst.	2
5	Instructional	3
6–11	Inst./Frust.	4–5
12 +	Frustration	6 +

Oral Reading Rate	Norm Group Percentile
⟌6720 WPM	☐ 90 ☐ 75 ☐ 50 ☐ 25 ☐ 10

Figure 2-4 Felipe's Performance on a Graded Passage

A 8224 (Grade 2)
Comprehension Questions

				Retelling/Notes

T   1. __+__   ¿De qué se trata el cuento?
(de un muchacho que <u>va camping</u>
con su familia)

F   2. __1/2__   ¿Le gustó a Jorge ir camping con
su familia? ¿Cómo sabes?
(le gustó; se puso contento)

Creo que sí. ¿Por qué sabes esto?
Lo dice.

F   3. __—__   ¿Por qué dieron un paseo Jorge y
su papá?
(para explorar el área)

para encontrar el perro de Jorge

F   4. __+__   ¿Qué clase de árboles encontraron?
(<u>pinos</u>; robles)

F   5. __+__   Además del ratón, ¿qué vio Jorge?
(<u>huellas</u> de animales; el nido de un
pájaro) *un nido*

F   6. __+__   ¿Dónde se metió el ratón?
(en un agujero)

I   7. __+__   ¿Por qué crees que el ratón se
metió en el agujero?
(cualquier respuesta lógica; quiso
esconderse; oyó a Jorge y sintió
miedo)

se escondió

I   8. __+__   ¿Por qué crees que Jorge y su papá
pensaron que las huellas eran de
animales?
(cualquier respuesta lógica)

eran pequeñas

E   9. __+__   ¿Qué otros animales crees que
Jorge podría encontrar si diera otro
paseo?
(cualquier respuesta lógica)

una culebra

V   10. __+__   ¿Qué son *huellas*?
(<u>donde se para un animal</u>; marcas
en la tierra; cualquier respuesta
lógica)

__1½__ Questions Missed

Comprehension Scoring Guide	
Questions Missed	Level
0–1	Independent
1½–2	Ind./Inst.
2½	Instructional
3–4½	Inst./Frust.
5 +	Frustration

Retelling
Excellent
Satisfactory
Unsatisfactory

Figure 2-5 Felipe's Performance on Comprehension Questions

Counting Significant Miscues

Determining the word recognition in context score by counting only significant miscues is a *qualitative* analysis of oral reading behavior. There is general agreement that certain substitutions, insertions, omissions, and the like do not seriously damage the student's understanding of the passage; hence, such miscues should not be counted as significant. Many teachers have also made similar observations.

> It must be remembered that accurate recognition is not the major objective in reading. *The goal is always meaning.* Because even proficient readers make errors on unfamiliar material, teachers must resist the temptation to meticulously correct all inconsequential mistakes. They must always ask whether a particular miscue really makes a difference (Goodman, 1971, p. 14).

It would appear that the best advice for counting significant miscues is to include those omissions, insertions, substitutions, mispronunciations, and other miscues that appear to affect comprehension. In short, significant miscues alter the meaning of the passage. The following method is suggested:

1. Count the **total** number of miscues in the passage.
2. Find the total of all dialect miscues, all corrected miscues, and all miscues that do not change the meaning.
3. Subtract this number from the total miscues. The result is the number of significant miscues.

The miscue chart provided with each graded passage makes it quite easy to determine the number, type, and significance of miscues.

Scoring Felipe's Oral Reading

From Felipe's oral reading of a second-grade passage, as recorded in Figure 2-4 on page 25, it is apparent that he made five total miscues. If you decided to count *total* miscues to determine Felipe's score in word recognition, you would record the numeral 5 in the "Total Miscues" box and circle the corresponding level (Instructional) in the Word Recognition Scoring Guide at the bottom of Figure 2-4. Then, the numeral and the level would be written on the summary sheet of the performance booklet. The same procedure would be used to determine the word recognition score for the other graded passages.

If you decided to count *significant* miscues, each of the five miscues would be evaluated within the context of the passage to determine whether the meaning of the passage was affected. After such an analysis, two of the miscues Felipe made (*explotar* and *ellas*) appear to be significant. There is a minor meaning change by omitting *robles* and substituting *corría* for *vieron* so each was counted as .5 so the total significant count for all the miscues would be three. You would record the numeral 3 in the "Significant Miscues" box and circle the corresponding level (Instructional) in the Word Recognition Scoring Guide. Then the numeral and the level would be recorded on the summary sheet of the performance booklet.

Figure 2-2 on page 19 contains various scores when the teacher decided to count *total* miscues. By consulting Table 2.2 on page 28 or the appropriate section of the Word Recognition Scoring Guide at the bottom of each passage, determine the reading levels that correspond to the various scores and place the appropriate levels in Figure 2-2. For example, at the pre-primer level, Felipe's *total* miscue count was 0. This score corresponds to a reading level of "Independent" which is written as *Ind.* in the appropriate column of Figure 2-2. For practice, write in the appropriate levels for primer, first, second, and third grade. Remember to use "Total Miscues" from the appropriate Word Recognition Scoring Guide on page 28.

Table 2.2

Scoring Guides for Words in Context (Total Miscues) for Form A, Grades 1–3

Word Recognition Scoring Guide, Grade 1			Word Recognition Scoring Guide, Grade 2			Word Recognition Scoring Guide, Grade 3		
Total Miscues	Level	Significant Miscues	Total Miscues	Level	Significant Miscues	Total Miscues	Level	Significant Miscues
0–1	Independent	0–1	0–1	Independent	0–1	0–1	Independent	0–1
2–4	Ind./Inst.	2	2–4	Ind./Inst.	2	2–4	Ind./Inst.	2
5	Instructional	3	5	Instructional	3	5	Instructional	3
6–9	Inst./Frust.	4	6–11	Inst./Frust.	4–5	6–9	Inst./Frust.	4
10 +	Frustration	5 +	12 +	Frustration	6 +	10 +	Frustration	5 +

Miscue counts of total and significant miscues may not always result in the same reading level. In such instances, reflect on the student's reading and use qualitative judgments to make the best possible appraisal. For example, a student may have a large miscue count that approaches frustration, but only a few of the uncorrected miscues result in a significant change in meaning. You may observe, however, that the student appears to be very nervous and frustrated. In addition, the student's rate of reading was quite labored and slow. Using this qualitative information will enable you to make a better judgment. In this example, it is doubtful that the passage was at the student's independent level. The passage is more likely instructional or frustration, depending on the student's comprehension.

Observation of Reading Behaviors and Other Evidence

In addition to counting miscues, pay attention to and note other evidence that may be helpful in determining the appropriateness of the passage for the student:

- finger pointing
- expression
- phrasing (good, adequate, poor)
- rate of reading in words per minute (WPM)
- flushed face or anxiety
- frustration
- guessing
- refusals
- sounds like English
- attitude
- persistence
- monitoring strategies
- background knowledge
- overall engagement

Teachers who use the Spanish Reading Inventory report that such behaviors and observations (qualitative data) are often as helpful as actual miscue counts and comprehension scores (quantitative data) in helping to determine whether a particular passage is easy, about right, or too difficult for the student. At the very least, these observations can provide additional information as tentative judgments are made regarding a student's oral reading and reading levels.

Determining Reading Levels from the Comprehension Questions or Retelling

The comprehension score is determined by counting the number of questions missed. To convert this score into one of the three reading levels, consult Table 2.3 or the scoring guide at the bottom of each passage. For example, if Felipe missed five comprehension questions, that passage would be at his frustration level.

The above procedure, however, is not directly applicable to the pre-primer passages, because they contain only five questions. Your judgment must be exercised in determining the student's comprehension score. If you decide that the score from the pre-primer levels did not accurately reflect the student's achievement, it would be permissible to place more emphasis on the score at the primer level when summarizing the results.

If you choose to use the retelling strategy to assess comprehension, you may (1) determine a percent score from the student's retelling or (2) identify the passage as one of the three reading levels without noting a specific percent of comprehension. You may also circle *excellent* (independent), *satisfactory* (instructional), or *unsatisfactory* (frustration) in the retelling box at the bottom of each graded passage in the performance booklet. The main point to keep in mind is whether the student's comprehension of the passage is judged to be at the independent, instructional, or frustration level.

Recording Felipe's Comprehension Scores for the Graded Passages

Figure 2-2 on page 19 contains Felipe's scores for the comprehension questions in the pre-primer through third-grade levels. By consulting Table 2.3 above or the scoring guide below each passage, determine the reading level that corresponds to each comprehension score and place these levels in Figure 2-2. When a student's scores fall between the reading levels, your judgment must be used. The recommended procedure is to record *Ind./Inst.* or *Inst./Frust.* on the summary sheet and circle the level closest to the actual score. If the score is exactly between two levels, circle the slash (/). The gray areas in the scoring guide indicate areas that require teacher judgment.

Determining Reading Levels—Silent Reading

Select a form of the Spanish Reading Inventory that the student did not read orally. **Begin the silent reading at the highest passage where the student achieved an independent level during oral reading.** If this procedure does not result in an independent level for silent reading, proceed to easier passages until an independent level is determined or the easiest pre-primer passage is read. Then, return to the original starting point and continue until the student reaches a frustration level.

As the student reads the passage silently, time the student's reading and note behavioral characteristics such as lip movement and finger pointing. Following silent reading, the passage is removed and the student's comprehension is assessed with comprehension questions, a retelling strategy, or a combination of the two.

The student continues to read increasingly difficult passages until a frustration level is determined. The various scores and corresponding reading levels should be entered at the appropriate place on the summary sheet. These silent reading levels can be used in conjunction with the student's oral reading performance to arrive at estimations of the three reading levels.

Table 2.3

Scoring Guide for Comprehension: Primer through Grade 8

Questions Missed	Level
0–1	Independent
1½–2	Ind./Inst.
2½	Instructional
3–4½	Inst./Frust.
5 +	Frustration

CAUTION!

TIP

TIP

Rate of Reading

A formula for determining a student's rate of reading is provided on the teacher copy of each graded-passage page in the performance booklet. The numeral in the $\overline{)}$ for each graded passage was determined by multiplying the number of words in the selection by sixty. This procedure permits the resulting division to be in words per minute (WPM). You can determine a student's rate of reading by using the formula provided. Merely record as the divisor of the formula the time (in seconds) the student takes to read the passage. Perform the necessary division, and the resulting numeral will be an estimate of the student's rate in words per minute (WPM). For example, suppose a student took 70 seconds to read the first-grade selection on Form A. You would divide 6,060 by 70. The result is a reading rate of approximately 86 words per minute (WPM).

$$\begin{array}{r} 86.5 \text{ WPM} \\ 70\overline{)6060} \\ \underline{560} \\ 460 \\ \underline{420} \\ 400 \\ \underline{350} \end{array}$$

Another way to determine words per minute is provided by the numerals at the end of each line of the teacher's passage (see Figure 2-6 below). These numerals represent the cumulative total of words to that point in the passage. Time the student's reading for one minute and draw a line or slash after the last word read by the student at the end of that minute. Then count the number of words not read on that line and subtract this numeral from the numeral at the end of the line. The result will be the number of words read in one minute. The line or slash in Figure 2-6 shows that the student read to the word *El* in one minute. By subtracting the six words not read from 81, the result is 75 words per minute (WPM).

Both of the above procedures determine words per minute (WPM). If you prefer to calculate words correct per minute (WCPM), the following may be done after one of the above procedures is used to determine WPM. Merely subtract the number of miscues made by the student from the WPM score. The result will be words correct per minute (WCPM). There are no universally accepted standards for which miscues to count. **It is recommended that mispronunciations, substitutions, omissions, and reversals be counted. Insertions, repetitions, and self-corrections are generally not counted in determining WCPM.** Using the example in Figure 2-6, there are four miscues: three substitutions and one omission. Following the above recommendations, three miscues (but not the insertion) would be subtracted from the total number of words read (75), resulting in 72 WCPM.

TIP

Jorge está en las Montañas

Era la primera vez que Jorge iba camping con	9
su familia. ¡Estaba tan contento de estar en las	18
montañas! En cuanto prepararon la casa de	25
campaña, él y su papá empezaron a *explotar* explorar el	34
área. Encontraron ~~robles~~ grandes, pinos	39
gigantes, y muchas clases de flores.	45
De pronto notaron unas pequeñas huellas que *ellas*	52
parecían ser de animales. Vieron un ratón que	60
se *cercaba* acercaba a un árbol y se metía en un pequeño	71
agujero de éste. El/ratón fue el único animal que *end of one minute*	81
vieron. Jorge sentía curiosidad por saber si todas	89
las huellas eran las del ratoncito. Lo último que	98
Jorge vio fue el nido de un pájaro en lo alto de	110
un árbol.	112

Figure 2-6 Example of a One-Minute Timed Reading

In addition, make general notes about a student's rate (for example, read very quickly; read slowly but accurately; seems to think that fast is best).

Norms for Oral and Silent Reading Rates

The norms in Table 2.4 on page 32 are based on four sources of information for students reading printed materials in English. There are currently no Spanish norms in the US for oral and silent reading rates. The first source was a five-year study by Forman and Sanders (1998) who established norms for first-grade students. Over 3,500 scores were obtained from students who took part in their study. These students were from a large suburban school district whose students generally score considerably above average on state and national reading assessments. Norms were provided for three points of the school year.

The second source was a study by Hasbrouck and Tindal (1992). Their study involved over 7,000 scores from students in grades two through five who read passages at sight for one minute from their grade-level texts, regardless of the students' instructional levels. Because most classrooms have students who represent a wide range of reading levels, their procedure resulted in some students reading passages that were very easy (independent level), while other students were asked to read passages that would be too difficult (frustration level). The norms provide words correct per minute (WCPM) at the 75th, 50th, and 25th percentiles for students in grades two through five at three points (fall, winter, and spring) in the school year.

The third source of data was reading fluency data that was gathered beginning in 1999 and ending with the 2002–2003 school year (www.edforamation.com). Over 240,000 scores for students in grades one through eight who read passages for one minute were analyzed. The passages were at grade level, which meant that they were easy for some students and difficult for other students. Separate norms were calculated for each of the four school years. The resulting norms for each year provide WCPM at the 90th, 75th, 50th, 25th, and 10th percentiles at three points (fall, winter, and spring) of the school year.

The fourth source of data was a follow-up study by Hasbrouck and Tindal (2006) using over 297,000 scores obtained from students in grades one through eight. Students represented all achievement levels, including those identified as gifted or reading disabled. English Language Learners (ELLs) who were receiving reading instruction in a regular classroom were also included in the data. Schools and districts from 23 states used curriculum-based measures (CBMs) for the assessment. This procedure resulted in some students reading materials at their frustration levels. Norms were compiled for students performing at the 90th, 75th, 50th, 25th, and 10th percentiles at three points throughout the school year (fall, winter, and spring) with the exception of grade one (which reported students' fluency norms for only the winter and spring).

All these data were thoughtfully studied, analyzed, and compiled into Table 2.4 by the authors using their professional judgment. The resulting table is intended to provide helpful information to those who desire to have some guidelines for students' reading rates. Because the norms are in words correct per minute (WCPM), comparing them to words per minute (WPM) as suggested in the Spanish Reading Inventory means that there is a slightly different basis for comparison. Comparisons can still be done and used to make informal appraisals regarding students' rates of reading. Just remember that the rates in Table 2.4 are more conservative than the rates determined by the WPM method. You can use the percentiles within each grade level to informally track and monitor student progress in rate throughout the school year.

In recent years, there has been mention of desired reading rates for various instructional levels or rate "targets" for students in various grades. Using the four sources of information previously described, Table 2.5 on page 33 was developed to provide rate "targets" for average students at three points in the school year (fall, winter, and spring). These figures are less than the "challenging" rates created by Carnine, Silbert, Kame'enui, and Tarver (2004, pp. 192–93) based on students who were performing very well on standardized tests. They argue that helping

Table 2.4

Oral Reading Norms for Students in Grades One through Eight

Grade (N)	Percentile	Fall N	Fall WCPM	Winter N	Winter WCPM	Spring N	Spring WCPM
1 (74,623)	90	2,847	32	33,366	75	38,410	105
	75		14		43		78
	50		7		22		50
	25		2		11		27
	10		1		6		14
2 (99,699)	90	29,634	102	33,683	124	36,382	141
	75		77		99		116
	50		50		72		89
	25		24		44		62
	10		12		19		34
3 (96,460)	90	29,832	128	32,371	145	34,257	161
	75		100		119		137
	50		72		91		107
	25		46		60		78
	10		24		36		47
4 (87,436)	90	29,609	144	27,373	165	30,454	180
	75		119		139		152
	50		94		111		124
	25		69		86		99
	10		42		60		72
5 (82,073)	90	28,510	165	25,229	181	28,334	194
	75		137		155		167
	50		109		126		138
	25		85		98		108
	10		60		73		81
6 (57,575)	90	18,923	177	17,668	194	20,984	204
	75		153		166		178
	50		127		140		150
	25		98		111		122
	10		67		81		93
7 (29,135)	90	10,687	176	7,313	188	11,135	200
	75		154		162		176
	50		127		134		150
	25		102		108		122
	10		79		86		97
8 (24,105)	90	8,674	183	5,986	193	9,445	198
	75		160		168		176
	50		130		142		151
	25		104		112		124
	10		79		84		97

N = number of student scores
WCPM = words correct per minute

Source: Jerry L. Johns and Susan Davis Lenski. *Improving Reading: Interventions, Strategies, and Resources* (5th ed.). Copyright © 2010 by Kendall Hunt Publishing Company.

From Jerry L. Johns and Mayra C. Daniel, *Spanish Reading Inventory: Pre-Primer through Grade Eight* (2nd ed.). Copyright © 2010 by Kendall Hunt Publishing Company (1-800-247-3458). May be reproduced for noncommercial educational purposes. Website: www.kendallhunt.com

students achieve high rates of fluency in the early grades leads to more reading by the student and makes school a more enjoyable experience. Keep in mind that the "targets" are best used to informally determine students' progress in comparison with so-called average students. Note in grade six and beyond that the target rate for the spring of the year levels at 150 words correct per minute. Because of individual differences in student ability and learning rates, expecting all students to reach a specific target is unrealistic.

Table 2.5
Mean Words Correct per Minute "Targets"* for Average Students in Grades One through Eight

Grade	Fall "Target"	Winter "Target"	Spring "Target"
1	Not Applicable	20	50
2	50	70	90
3	70	90	110
4	95	110	125
5	110	125	140
6	125	140	150
7	125	140	150
8	130	140	150

*The "targets" are reported in "round" numbers.

Carver (1989, p. 165) has provided information on *silent* reading rates for students in grades one through eight that "may be helpful to teachers who administer informal reading inventories." The figures he presents are the average rates of students in that *particular* grade who can *understand* material at *that* grade level. Although Carver's figures are in standard word lengths, they may be useful as a rough indication of the average rates at which average students in a particular grade read with understanding. These rates are based on students reading English. Users of the Spanish Reading Inventory, then, can use the figures presented in Table 2.6 when evaluating a student's silent reading ability.

Table 2.6
Silent Reading Rates for Students in Various Grades Who Understand the Material

Grade	1	2	3	4	5	6	7	8
WPM	<81	82–108	109–130	131–147	148–161	162–174	175–185	186–197

The Listening Level

In addition to the three reading levels, you may wish to get a rough estimate of the student's listening level or potential for substantial growth in reading. Intelligence tests are sometimes used to estimate potential for reading; however, their limitations have led some teachers to read graded passages to a student and determine the highest level of material that the student can understand. Undertaking such a procedure is known as determining the student's listening level. This procedure should **not** be used with students in the primary grades (Schell, 1982).

CAUTION!

Determining the Listening Level

Select a form of the Spanish Reading Inventory that was not used. The listening level is determined after *you* read increasingly difficult passages to the student. Start by reading the title and developing a purpose for listening to the passage. When you read, pronounce the words carefully so that your own dialect of Spanish is not a factor in the student's aural comprehension.

Procedures similar to those suggested earlier may be used: Invite the student to predict what the passage will be about and then have the student *listen* to the content in the passage as you read it *to* the student. After the passage has been read, assess the student's comprehension with the questions, a retelling strategy, or a combination of the two. The criteria for estimating the student's listening level is a comprehension score of three or fewer questions missed. You should also informally note the student's ability to use vocabulary and language structures as complex as those used in the passage read.

It is recommended that you begin reading a passage that is not higher than the student's instructional level. Then continue reading more difficult passages until the student misses more than three comprehension questions. The *highest* passage at which the student misses three or fewer questions is his or her listening level.

Scoring Juan's Listening Level

Suppose, for example, that Juan is a fifth-grade student who has a fourth-grade instructional level and you wish to determine his listening level or potential. Choose a passage at the fourth-grade level from a form of the Spanish Reading Inventory that Juan has not read. After reading the passage aloud, ask and have Juan respond to the comprehension questions. If Juan misses three or fewer questions, continue reading increasingly difficult passages until he misses more than three questions. The highest level at which Juan meets this criterion is identified as his listening level. To illustrate this procedure, consider the data in Table 2.7.

Table 2.7
Data for Juan's Listening Level

Level of Passage	Comprehension Questions Missed
4 (B 5414)	0
5 (B 8595)	2
6 (B 6867)	3
7 (B 3717)	4

Based on these data, Juan's listening level would be sixth grade, because that was the highest level at which he missed three or fewer questions. Because his listening level (sixth grade) is higher than his instructional level (fourth grade), you would have reason to believe that Juan has the potential to increase his reading ability. Harris and Sipay (1990) suggest a two-year discrepancy between the listening level and the instructional level as a rough criterion for practical significance. In this instance, Juan's listening comprehension can be viewed as a favorable prognostic sign; namely, Juan should be able to understand material at the sixth-grade level once he acquires the necessary reading competence.

CAUTION!

There are some limitations for using the listening level as an indicator of reading potential. Consider the listening level as a rough estimate of reading potential that needs to be supported from observation, your familiarity with the student's background, and the results of measures of intellectual capacity.

Figure 2-7 provides a summary of procedures for administering and scoring the Spanish Reading Inventory.

Spanish Reading Inventory Administration and Scoring Procedures

To determine a student's independent, instructional, and frustration levels, administer the graded word lists and graded passages included in the Spanish Reading Inventory as follows:

WORD RECOGNITION IN ISOLATION: Select a graded word list at a reading level that will be easy for the student. Ask the student to pronounce the words at a comfortable rate. Record the student's responses in the sight column beside the corresponding word list in the performance booklet.

Return to mispronounced or unknown words for an attempt at analysis and note the student's responses in the analysis column. Administer successive word lists until the student is no longer able to achieve a **total** score of at least 14 correct words or until the student becomes frustrated.

Scoring: Total the correct responses in the sight and analysis columns. Consult the criteria on the scoring guide at the bottom of the word lists to determine a rough estimate of the reading level achieved on each graded word list. Record the number-correct scores and the reading levels on the summary sheet of the performance booklet.

WORD RECOGNITION IN CONTEXT: Ask the student to read aloud the passage graded at least one level below the highest independent level achieved on the graded word lists. If desired, time the student's reading. As the student reads the passage, record all miscues such as omissions, repetitions, substitutions, and the like on the corresponding copy of the passage found in the performance booklet.

Scoring: Count the number of total miscues or significant miscues (those that affect meaning) in each graded passage.

To determine reading levels from the word recognition in context scores, consult the criteria on the scoring guide at the bottom of the passage. Record the score and the reading levels on the summary sheet of the performance booklet.

COMPREHENSION: Ask the comprehension questions that accompany the passage in the performance booklet and record the student's responses. Continue administering graded passages until the student has many word recognition miscues or is unable to answer half the comprehension questions. Also, watch for behavior associated with frustration: lack of expression, word-by-word reading, excessive anxiety, and so on.

Scoring: Count the number of comprehension questions missed.

To convert these scores into reading levels, consult the criteria on the scoring guide at the bottom of the questions. (Teacher judgment must be exercised at the pre-primer levels because the limited number of questions may not permit precise measurement of achievement.) Record the scores and the reading levels on the summary sheet of the performance booklet.

Figure 2-7 Administration and Scoring Procedures

Determining the Student's Three Reading Levels and Instructional Uses

Assimilating the Results

After you have summarized the results for graded word lists, words in context, and passage comprehension, estimates of the student's independent level, instructional level, and frustration level can be determined. Figure 3-1 contains a summary of Felipe's performance on Form A of the Spanish Reading Inventory. The various scores and levels should correspond to your efforts to complete the examples that were presented in Figure 2-2 on page 19. Check your results from Figure 2-2 with Figure 3-1 and resolve any discrepancies.

Grade	Word Recognition						Comprehension		Reading Rate	
	Isolation (Word Lists)				Context (Passages)		Oral Reading Form A			
	Sight	Analysis	Total	Level	Miscues*	Level	Questions Missed	Level	Words per Minute (WPM)	Norm Group Percentile
PP2	16	3	19	Ind.	0	Ind.	0	Ind.		
P	16	1	17	Inst.	1	Ind.	½	Ind.		
1	16	1	17	Inst.	2	Ind./Inst.	0	Ind.		
2	14	2	16	Inst.	5	Inst.	1½	Ind./Inst.		
3	10	2	12	Frust.	12	Frust.	5	Frust.		

*Refers to *total* miscues in this example

Figure 3-1 Summary of Felipe's Performance on Form A of the Spanish Reading Inventory

From the data presented in Figures 2-2 and 3-1, it would appear that Felipe's independent levels are pre-primer (PP2), primer (P), and first grade. Because the independent level is the *highest* level at which Felipe can read books by himself, first grade would be his independent level. Materials at the second-grade level of difficulty should be appropriate for instruction. At this level Felipe should make maximum progress under teacher guidance. The third-grade level, according to the criteria, appears to be his frustration level. In summary, Felipe's three reading levels are: independent—first grade, instructional—second grade, and frustration—third grade.

It should be noted that most summary sheets, unlike Figure 3-1, will not provide clear distinctions among the three reading levels. When discrepancies arise, use judgment in determining the student's three levels. You should consider the student's performance *preceding* and *following* the level in question, as well as the student's performance *within* a particular level.

TIP

Generally, the recommended procedure is to place greater emphasis on comprehension. **Remember that the goal of reading is constructing meaning from print.** The ability to pronounce words *is* important; nevertheless, word identification must always be judged with regard to the student's ability to understand the passage. In making decisions, **place emphasis first on comprehension** (both oral and silent), then word recognition in *context*, and finally word recognition in *isolation*. In addition, give greater emphasis to silent reading comprehension in the upper grades.

It is also important to consider the behaviors of the student at each reading level to aid in proper placement. A student's scores, for example, may suggest the ability to read independently at a certain level of difficulty; however, the student may appear to be quite nervous and exhibit behavior suggesting that such a level is too difficult for independent reading. Exercise extreme care in determining a student's three reading levels. It is always best to give a student easier material than to give or recommend a book to the student that might be difficult and frustrating.

In most cases, the three reading levels serve as a starting point for high-quality reading instruction. Because the reading levels are determined in a relatively short period of time, they should be regarded as estimates. Do not consider a student's three reading levels to be rigid and static. If, in working with the student, you find that the student's various reading levels are not accurate, the necessary adjustments should be made. Keep in mind that the passages in the Spanish Reading Inventory provide a limited sample of student reading behavior. Adjustments, based on classroom performance and observations, should be made when necessary.

Estimating Mario's Three Reading Levels

Interpreting the summary of Mario's reading, presented in Figure 3-2, requires some teacher judgment. Note that *total* miscues are recorded for word recognition in context.

| Grade | Word Recognition | | | | | | Comprehension | | Reading Rate | |
| | Isolation (Word Lists) | | | | Context (Passages) | | Oral Reading | | | |
	Sight	Analysis	Total	Level	Miscues*	Level	Questions Missed	Level	Words per Minute (WPM)	Norm Group Percentile
1	20	0	20	Ind.	1	Ind.	1	Ind.		
2	19	1	20	Ind.	4	Ind./Inst.	1	Ind.		
3	14	2	16	Inst.	5	Inst.	2½	Inst.		
4	11	2	13	Inst./Frust.	8	Inst./Frust.	6	Frust.		

*Refers to *total* miscues in this example

Figure 3-2 Summary of Mario's Performance on the Spanish Reading Inventory

All the scores for the first- and third-grade levels present no problems, because the numerals correspond to a single reading level. At the second-grade level, however, Mario's word recognition in context is below the criteria for a clear independent level. Because Mario's other two scores at the second-grade level are marked independent, you could hypothesize that second grade is probably his independent level. For the fourth-grade level, Mario achieved the instructional/frustration level for words in isolation and word recognition in context. His score for comprehension is at the frustration level. Mario is unable to comprehend the material satisfactorily, so fourth grade is probably Mario's frustration level. Now, by analyzing Mario's performance *within* a given level and *between* the four levels, you can verify earlier hypotheses and make a judgment that his three reading levels are: independent—second grade, instructional—third grade, and frustration—fourth grade.

It is possible for some students to have a range of grades within the instructional level. If, for example, Mario's scores in Figure 3-2 were changed so that the comprehension score at the second-grade level was 2 questions missed, his three reading levels would probably be: independent—first grade, instructional—second grade and third grade, and frustration—fourth grade. Given a range of instructional levels, where should Mario be placed for instruction? The recommended procedure is to place him in second-grade reading materials and carefully monitor his progress. If he does well at this level, third-grade reading materials could be tried. Generally, it is easier to move a student to a higher level than to a lower level.

Estimating Pablo's Three Reading Levels

Another summary sheet that requires judgment is shown in Figure 3-3. Study the percentages and make a judgment with regard to Pablo's independent, instructional, and frustration levels before continuing. Note that **significant** miscues are recorded for word recognition in context.

At the primer level, resolve Pablo's word recognition score in context. Two significant miscues could be either independent or instructional; however, by examining the other scores *within* that level, you should judge primer as his independent level because of his near-perfect scores in these areas. The first-grade level requires judgment in oral reading comprehension. Because the score in comprehension is near the independent level (one or fewer questions missed) and the other three scores within this level are independent, you should conclude that the first-grade level is also independent. At the second-grade level, the two significant miscues for word recognition in context is probably best identified as instructional because Pablo's other three scores are instructional.

The third-grade level requires judgment for words in isolation, word recognition in context, and oral reading comprehension. All of these scores appear to be nearer the frustration level, so a tentative judgment for the third-grade level is frustration. Little judgment is required at the fourth-grade level because all scores are clearly frustration. In addition, because the third-grade level was judged to be frustration, the fourth-grade level, by definition, would also be frustration.

Grade	Word Recognition						Comprehension				Reading Rate	
	Isolation (Word Lists)				Context (Passages)		Oral Reading Form A		Silent Reading Form B		Words per Minute (WPM)	Norm Group Percentile
	Sight	Analysis	Total	Level	Miscues*	Level	Questions Missed	Level	Questions Missed	Level		
P	20	0	20	Ind.	2	Ind./Inst.	0	Ind.	1	Ind.		
1	19	1	20	Ind.	1	Ind.	1½	Ind./Inst.	1	Ind.		
2	16	2	18	Inst.	2	Ind./Inst.	2½	Inst.	2½	Inst.		
3	14	1	15	Inst./Frust.	4	Inst./Frust.	4½	Inst./Frust.	5	Frust.		
4	12	1	13	Frust.	6	Frust.	5	Frust.	6	Frust.		

*Refers to *significant* miscues in this example

Figure 3-3 Summary of Pablo's Performance on Form A and Form B of the Spanish Reading Inventory

Decide on Pablo's reading levels using Figure 3-3 above. From the earlier judgments, his three reading levels would probably be independent—first grade, instructional—second grade, and frustration—third grade.

Determining Word Identification Strategies

Any system of analyzing the student's word identification strategies should be guided by a careful and thoughtful analysis of oral reading performance. Conrad and Shankin (1999) suggest helpful ways to use miscues to understand the student's reading. In addition, Johnson, Kress, and Pikulski (1987) provide several questions that may help guide the overall analysis:

● Does the student's oral reading reflect a balanced use of sight vocabulary, context clues, phonics, structural analysis, and syntactic clues? Do weaknesses appear to exist in any of these areas?

● Is the student's oral reading fluent or is the student's reading hesitant or read word by word?

● To what extent do the student's miscues alter or interfere with the meaning of the passages read?

● When miscues occur, does the student appear to be monitoring his or her reading by rereading, correcting unacceptable miscues (those that adversely affect meaning), and/or noting that the passage is difficult? Are the miscues influenced by the student's dialect or language background?

● Does the student's limited vocabulary, background, or concept development appear to be affecting oral reading?

● Do any patterns emerge by analyzing the student's miscues and oral reading behavior?

Miscue Analysis Total

The teacher's passages in the Spanish Reading Inventory have provisions to total miscues and other reading behaviors as shown in Figure 3-4 on page 41. The totals should be completed *after* the assessment session with the student has been completed.

The example in Figure 3-4 on the following page is based on Felipe's oral reading in Figure 2-4 (page 25). Each miscue should be considered and tallied accordingly. Felipe substituted *explotar* for *explorar,* so a 1 is placed in the substitution column. Because this miscue resulted in a meaning change, a tally mark is also placed under the meaning change column. The same columns were also marked for the miscue *ellas* because it was a substitution miscue that also changed the meaning. The miscue *robles* is an omission, so a 1 is placed in the omission column on the appropriate line of the text. The teacher judged that this miscue was a minor change in meaning, so half (.5) was placed in the meaning change column. The same reasoning was used for *corría.* The miscue *cercaba* for *acercaba* was a substitution that the teacher felt did not result in a significant meaning change; therefore, a 1 was only placed in the substitution column corresponding to the line of text where the miscue was made.

Once the totals for miscues and other reading behaviors are completed for the appropriate passages read by the student, they can be summarized on the two sample charts shown in Figure 3-5 on page 42. These charts are also contained in Appendix A for your reproduction and use.

After completing the Miscue Total and Reading Behavior Summary Charts for your students, look for patterns in order to hypothesize areas where the student might profit from strategy lessons. In the sample charts shown in Figure 3-5, the student has a large number of omissions. You might offer responsive instruction for omissions. The student in this example also corrected a number of miscues that changed the meaning. Behavior of this sort should be seen as a reading strength, and the student should be praised for monitoring reading and using correction strategies. Some effort should be made to increase the student's sight vocabulary to build greater automaticity with words encountered during reading.

Student Copy is on page 62.

A 8224 (Grade 2) Activating Background: Lee el título a ti mismo. Luego dime qué crees que va a pasar en el cuento.

Background: Low ├───────┼───────┤ High

Jorge está en las Montañas

		MISCUES					
	Substitution	Insertion	Omission	Reversal	Repetition	Self-Correction of Unacceptable Miscue	Meaning Change (Significant Miscue)
Era la primera vez que Jorge iba camping con — 9							
su familia. ¡Estaba tan contento de estar en las — 18							
montañas! En cuanto prepararon la casa de — 25							
campaña, él y su papá empezaron a *explotar* explorar el — 34	1						1
área. Encontraron ~~robles~~ grandes, pinos — 39			1				.5
gigantes, y muchas clases de flores. — 45							
De pronto notaron unas pequeñas huellas que *ellas* — 52	1						1
parecían ser de animales. Vieron un ratón que — 60							
se acercaba a un árbol y se metía en un pequeño *cercaba* — 71	1						
agujero de éste. El ratón fue el único animal que — 81							
vieron. Jorge sentía curiosidad por saber si todas *corría* — 89	1						.5
las huellas eran las del ratoncito. Lo último que — 98							
Jorge vio fue el nido de un pájaro en lo alto de — 110							
un árbol. — 112							
TOTAL	4	0	1	0			3

Total Miscues [5]   Significant Miscues [3]

Word Recognition Scoring Guide

Total Miscues	Level	Significant Miscues
0–1	Independent	0–1
2–4	Ind./Inst.	2
5	Instructional	3
6–11	Inst./Frust.	4–5
12 +	Frustration	6 +

Oral Reading Rate	Norm Group Percentile
___ WPM /)6720	☐ 90 ☐ 75 ☐ 50 ☐ 25 ☐ 10

Figure 3-4 Felipe's Miscue Tally on a Graded Passage

Total Miscues Across Passages Read	Type of Miscue			
	Substitution	**Insertion**	**Omission**	**Reversal**
	3	*2*	*8*	*0*

Other Reading Behaviors (Totals)	**Repetition**	**Self-Correction of Unacceptable Miscues**	**Meaning Change**
	2	*6*	*2*

Figure 3-5 Sample Miscue Total and Reading Behavior Summary Charts

Analyzing Comprehension

To guide the overall assessment of the student's comprehension, the following questions should be considered:

- Does the student appear to know that comprehension is the goal of reading?
- Does the student appear to possess the background (concepts and vocabulary) necessary for understanding the passage?
- Are there significant differences between the student's oral and silent comprehension?
- Do significant comprehension differences exist between narrative and expository passages?
- Are there significant differences in comprehension between the shorter passages and the longer passages?
- Does the student appear to have difficulties with specific types of comprehension questions?
- What does the student do when comprehension becomes difficult?
- Does the student monitor his or her reading and use appropriate fix-up strategies?

TIP

The Spanish Reading Inventory contains five different types of comprehension questions coded as follows: (F) fact, (T) topic, (E) evaluation, (I) inference, and (V) vocabulary. When analyzing a student's comprehension performance, **only comprehension questions at the student's independent, instructional, and instructional/frustration levels should be used**. Comprehension questions at the student's frustration level may be used to verify tendencies at the student's independent and instructional levels.

Lest you glibly use the classification scheme suggested, it must be emphasized that these categories of comprehension questions, although widely used, have little or no empirical support (Schell & Hanna, 1981). In other words, many reading tests claim to measure comprehension skills that authorities cannot show to exist. Although such analysis lacks empirical support, Johnson, Kress, and Pikulski (1987) believe such a procedure is useful to help identify general tendencies in comprehension. Spache (1976) notes that comprehension is composed of three essential elements: (1) a word meaning factor, (2) a relationships-among-ideas factor, and (3) a reasoning factor. He goes on to say that "when the reading teacher has determined by repeated observations that the student apparently does not use a certain type of essential thinking, the remedial course is quite obvious. She may repeatedly ask the student to attempt to answer questions that appear to sample the missing cognitive process" (p. 269). The following strategy described for determining strengths and weaknesses in comprehension offer a systematic way for you to gather preliminary evidence indicating that some aspect of a student's comprehension may need attention. You can then support or refute this tentative need through the student's performance in classroom activities. If a need exists, you can develop appropriate interventions and strategy lessons. Remember that the scheme for analyzing comprehension performance is intended to be used informally. It should aid your judgment, not replace it.

CAUTION!

Analysis of Comprehension by Question Type

You can analyze comprehension after recording the number and types of questions the student misses on each passage read at the independent, instructional, and instructional/frustration levels. An example of this procedure, using Roberto's comprehension scores, is shown in Figure 3-6. A reproducible master for your use is found in Appendix A. Using such a procedure may enable you to discern patterns of possible difficulty in comprehension. Roberto's performance on the comprehension questions marked in Figure 3-6 indicates possible strengths in answering topic and vocabulary questions. Areas of possible weakness include answering fact, evaluation, and inference questions. Because of the limited data upon which these hypotheses are based, Roberto's silent reading should also be considered. These hypotheses should then be verified or discounted through observation and ongoing instruction.

Grade	Fact (F-6)* Oral	Topic (T-1) Oral	Evaluation (E-1) Oral	Inference (I-1) Oral	Vocabulary (V-1) Oral
P	2 /6	0 /1	0 /1	0 /1	0 /1
1	1 /6	0 /1	0 /1	0 /1	0 /1
2	3 /6	0 /1	0 /1	1 /1	0 /1
3	2 /6	0 /1	1 /1	1 /1	0 /1
Ratio Missed	8 / 24	0 / 4	1 / 4	2 / 4	0 / 4
Percent Missed	33 %	0 %	25 %	50 %	0 %

*Indicates the type of question and the number of questions in each graded paragraph. For example, F indicates a fact question and 6 signifies that each graded passage contains six F questions.

Figure 3-6 Summary of Roberto's Comprehension Performance in Oral Reading

Next, consider Gilberto's errors on the comprehension questions. To determine Gilberto's tendencies in comprehension, complete Figure 3-7 by determining the ratios of comprehension questions missed and the corresponding percentages. First, record the number of questions missed for each question type. Second, determine the percent of errors by dividing the number of errors by the total number of that question type and multiplying by 100. For example, Gilberto responded to 30 fact questions and missed 4 of them. His error rate for the fact questions was 13 percent (4 ÷ 30 = .13; .13 × 100 = 13%). What are Gilberto's possible strengths and weaknesses in comprehension?

During oral reading, Gilberto missed 4 of 30 fact questions (13%), 3 of 5 topic questions (60%), 2 of 5 evaluation questions (40%), 1 of 5 inference questions (20%), and 2 of 5 vocabulary questions (40%). Based on these percentages, answering topic questions may be hypothesized as an area of weakness. A possible strength is in the area of recalling facts. It seems most appropriate from this analysis to identify errors in topic questions as a possible weakness and responses to fact questions as a possible strength. Whether the areas of evaluation, inference,

Grade	Fact (F-6) Oral	Topic (T-1) Oral	Evaluation (E-1) Oral	Inference (I-1) Oral	Vocabulary (V-1) Oral
4	_1_/6	_0_/1	_0_/1	_0_/1	_0_/1
5	_0_/6	_0_/1	_1_/1	_1_/1	_0_/1
6	_1_/6	_1_/1	_0_/1	_0_/1	_0_/1
7	_0_/6	_1_/1	_0_/1	_0_/1	_1_/1
8	_2_/6	_1_/1	_1_/1	_0_/1	_1_/1
Ratio Missed	_4_/_30_	__/__	__/__	__/__	__/__
Percent Missed	_13_%	__%	__%	__%	__%

Figure 3-7 Gilberto's Comprehension Performance in Oral Reading

and vocabulary warrant instructional intervention should be based on additional information gained from classroom observations and relevant performance on reading tasks. Table 3.1 contains the completed analysis of Gilberto's comprehension performance so you can compare your results.

Table 3.1
Summary of Gilberto's Comprehension Performance in Oral Reading

	Fact	Topic	Evaluation	Inference	Vocabulary
Ratio Missed	4/30	3/5	2/5	1/5	2/5
Percent Missed	13%	60%	40%	20%	40%

Fluency Considerations

The Spanish Reading Inventory offers an excellent means to gain insights into the student's reading fluency. The Report of the National Reading Panel (2000) identified fluency as one of the foundational areas for reading instruction. Fluency has several components, aspects, or elements (Harris & Hodges, 1995; Samuels, 2002). Johns and Berglund (2010) note that fluency is comprised of four components: rate, accuracy, expression, and comprehension. How you can gain insights in each of these four areas is explained below.

Rate refers to speed of reading. When the student begins reading a graded passage orally or silently, you can time the student's reading using a stopwatch or a watch with a second hand. There are two ways you can determine the student's rate or speed of reading. These two methods are described in detail on pages 30–33. In short, the first method determines the number of seconds it takes the student to read the passage and uses the formula at the bottom of the passage to get the student's rate in words per minute (WPM). Then the student's rate can be compared to the norms in Table 2.4 on page 32. Figure 3-8 contains an example for Vince, a third-grade student in the fall of grade three.

Oral Reading Rate	Norm Group Percentile
$\dfrac{52}{120\,)\overline{6240}}$ WPM	☐ 90 ☐ 75 ☐ 50 ☒ 25 ☐ 10

Figure 3-8 Vince's Oral Reading Rate

The second way to determine reading rate is described on page 30. The teacher who uses that method determines the student's reading for one minute and draws a line or slash after the last word read by the student at the end of one minute. An example of this procedure is shown in Figure 2-6 (page 30).

Once the student's oral rate of reading is determined with either of these methods, consult Table 2.4 (page 32) and check the percentile that most closely corresponds to the student's rate in WPM. Table 2.5 (page 33) could also be used to help determine how the student's reading rate compares to average students at various points in the school year. For Vince, it can be seen that his rate is near the 25th percentile when the teacher compared his rate on a third-grade passage in the fall of the school year. Figure 3-8 shows Vince's reading rate (52 WPM) and approximate percentile rank (25).

Accuracy refers to the facility with which the student recognizes words. In terms of the Spanish Reading Inventory, the word recognition in context score gives some indication of the student's automaticity with words. You can also observe the student's ability to pronounce words and the ease with which the student reads the passage. Obviously, a student who makes many miscues (misses one word in ten) would likely be trying to read a passage that is too difficult. The word lists can also be used to assess the student's ability to pronounce words at sight (automatically).

Appropriate expression means that the student uses phrasing, tone, and pitch so that oral reading sounds conversational (Johns & Berglund, 2010). As the student reads, you can note the appropriateness of the oral reading in flow, emphasis, and phrasing. There are also more formal fluency rubrics that can be used if desired (see Johns & Berglund, 2010; Johns, Berglund, & L'Allier, 2007).

Comprehension is the essence of reading and refers to understanding the passage. Comprehension of passages on the Spanish Reading Inventory is typically assessed with questions, retelling, or a combination of the two. Without comprehension, the student is merely word calling. There are some students who are very good at pronouncing words who are not actively constructing meaning. On the surface, these students may seem like excellent readers because they sound so good. Unfortunately, these readers are really automatic word callers (Valencia & Buly, 2004).

Important Points to Remember about Fluency

Fluency is dependent upon a variety of factors; the most important is probably an adequate sight vocabulary. Slow, choppy reading can be the result of not knowing a number of the words in the passage. It has been noted that "inefficiency in identifying individual words is the most important factor in accounting for individual differences in text reading fluency in samples of students with reading disabilities" (Torgesen, 2004, p. 376). Viewed from this perspective, fluency is symptomatic of poor reading rather than the cause of it. Many students improve their fluency when they are given books to read where they can recognize approximately 95 percent of the words. The interest and background the student has about the topic or content of the reading material can also impact fluency.

If a student's reading is not fluent, hypothesize the most basic reasons for the behavior. Those hypotheses should then be used as the basis for initial responsive instruction. For example, one student may have weak word identification skills and a limited sight vocabulary. These areas would be the logical focus for instruction. Another student may have accurate, slow reading with adequate comprehension. For this student, instruction to increase rate may be appropriate. A third student may use improper phrasing and ignore punctuation.

Through experience with the Spanish Reading Inventory and a careful analysis of the student's reading, you will learn to differentiate the need for instruction in fluency from other, more causal factors for the lack of fluent reading (e.g., limited sight vocabulary and inadequate skills for word identification). It should also be noted that after third grade, the number of less frequent words increases rapidly, so it is difficult for students who struggle in reading to catch up with average students (Torgesen, 2004). Many of these students would likely profit from focused instruction in needed areas and extensive periods of practice that exceeds that of average students.

Instructional Interventions Chart

To help you make instruction more responsive to the student's needs based on the results of the Spanish Reading Inventory, classroom observations, and the student's daily work, there are numerous sources for ideas. Several easy-to-use strategy books to help in your quest to enhance student achievement in reading are described below.

Improving Reading: Interventions, Strategies, and Resources (Johns & Lenski, 2010) contains a wealth of teaching strategies and interventions (over 200), practice and reinforcement activities (over 400), games, and over 200 reproducible materials to use with students. The ideas in this resource book support a wide range of readers. A Quick Reference Guide on the inside cover is keyed to 69 student behaviors in reading along with appropriate interventions and strategies. Teachers from kindergarten through high school have used the strategies to energize their instruction with average students as well as with students who struggle in reading. The fifth edition of *Improving Reading* contains more strategies than earlier editions and has many resource materials that can be duplicated and readily used with students. A CD makes it even easier to use the reproducibles (over 200) and resources. Refer to the instructional interventions chart on page 47 (Figure 3-9) for a comprehensive overview of the areas included in *Improving Reading*.

Teaching Reading Pre-K–Grade 3 (Elish-Piper, Johns, & Lenski, 2006) contains 28 different assessments in areas such as literacy knowledge, phoneme segmentation, phonics, decoding, retelling, sight words, fluency, passage reading, and writing. These assessments can be used with students who are emergent readers up to third grade. A unique feature of the book is the presentation of over 300 teaching strategies, ideas, and activities that are linked to the assessments. Also included are ideas to send home to help practice and reinforce needed skills and strategies. These home-school connections are presented in English and Spanish. A number of tips for English language learners are highlighted in an easy-to-use chart. To make this resource even easier to use, a CD is included. It contains a bonus chapter on writing and spelling, 40 instructional reproducibles, home-school connections, selected resources, and assessment record sheets.

Comprehension and Vocabulary Strategies for the Elementary Grades (Johns, Lenski, & Berglund, 2006) contains over 40 comprehension and vocabulary strategies neatly organized with a quick reference guide that shows when, why, and how to use the strategies. Also shown is the type of text (narrative and/or informational) with which the strategy is most useful. Teaching is enhanced with a step-by-step lesson format and numerous examples. Reproducible masters, which you can use for instructional purposes, are provided with each strategy. A CD contains over 120 of these reproducibles plus bonus reproducibles for selected strategies.

Fluency: Differentiated Interventions and Progress-Monitoring Assessments (Johns & Berglund, 2010) provides answers to questions teachers often ask about fluency and over 30 strategies

Interventions Chart for Responsive and Differentiated Instruction

General Area Specific Interventions	Resource Book *Improving Reading* (5th ed.)	General Area Specific Interventions	Resource Book *Improving Reading* (5th ed.)
1. Motivation, Engagement, Interests, and Attitudes		**4. Fluency and Effective Oral Reading** *(continued)*	
Lack of Motivation and Engagement	1.1	Lack of Expression	4.5
Negative Attitude Toward Reading	1.2	Overemphasis on Speed and Accuracy	4.6
Limited Reading Interests	1.3	Failure to Attempt Unknown Words	4.7
Low Confidence in Reading Ability	1.4	Meaning-Changing Substitutions	4.8
Reluctant to Set Goals	1.5	Nonmeaning-Changing Substitutions	4.9
		Nonword Substitutions	4.10
2. Oral Language, Phonemic Awareness, and Beginning Reading		Meaning-Changing Omissions	4.11
Oral Language	2.1	Nonmeaning-Changing Omissions	4.12
Concepts About the Nature and Purpose of Reading	2.2	Excessive Use of Phonics	4.13
Alphabet Knowledge	2.3	Excessive Use of Experience	4.14
Auditory Discrimination	2.4	**5. Vocabulary Development and Extension**	
Concept of a Word	2.5	Extending Meaning Vocabulary	5.1
Rhyming	2.6	Differentiating Between Word Meanings	5.2
Syllabic Awareness	2.7	Speaking and Writing Vocabulary	5.3
Alphabetic Principle	2.8	Using Context Clues to Predict Meanings of Unknown Words	5.4
Onsets and Rimes	2.9	Compound Words and Affixes	5.5
Phonemic Awareness	2.10	Dictionary: Word Meanings	5.6
Visual Discrimination	2.11	Interest in Words	5.7
Letter and Word Reversals	2.12	**6. Comprehension Skills**	
Sense of Story	2.13	Previewing Text	6.1
3. Phonics, Decoding, and Word Identification		Activating Prior Knowledge	6.2
Phonics: Consonants	3.1	Lack of Clear Purpose(s) for Reading	6.3
Phonics: Vowels	3.2	Main Point or Idea	6.4
Word Patterns and Word Building	3.3	Facts or Details	6.5
Structural Analysis	3.4	Sequence	6.6
Basic Sight (High-Frequency) Words	3.5	Making Predictions	6.7
Sight Vocabulary	3.6	Making Inferences	6.8
Using Context to Predict Known Words	3.7	Visualizing	6.9
Dictionary: Word Pronunciation	3.8	Drawing Conclusions	6.10
Lack of Flexible Word-Identification Strategies	3.9	**7. Comprehension Strategies**	
Ineffective Use of Word-Identification Strategies	3.10	Understanding Fictional Text Structure	7.1
4. Fluency and Effective Oral Reading		Understanding Informational Text Structure	7.2
General Lack of Fluency	4.1	Charts and Graphs	7.3
Lack of Fluency: Poor Phrasing	4.2	Inflexible Rate of Reading	7.4
Lack of Fluency: Ignoring Punctuation	4.3	Monitoring Reading	7.5
Lack of Fluency: Repetitions of Words or Phrases	4.4	Summarizing Ideas	7.6
		Making Connections	7.7
		Processing Text	7.8
		Evaluating Written Materials	7.9
		Remembering	7.10

Figure 3-9 Interventions Chart

to strengthen fluency that are keyed to six reader types. A brief description is provided for each strategy, followed by a numbered set of procedures on how to use the strategy with students. Narrative and informational passages for progress monitoring in fluency in grades one through eight are also included.

Visualization: Using Mental Images to Strengthen Comprehension (Zeigler & Johns, 2005) offers answers to some basic questions about visualization and provides 60 lessons to help students realize what visualization is, understand how to use it, and then apply it in various subject areas. Also included are assessments with scoring rubrics.

Strategies for Content Area Learning: Vocabulary, Comprehension, and Response (Johns & Berglund, 2006) contains over 30 strategies, each accompanied with a reproducible. The strategies can be used with narrative and/or informational text. Like the other books described above, the lessons are well organized and presented in easy-to-use steps. In addition to some readily recognized strategies (like K-W-L), there are less well known, but effective, strategies (for example, concept circles, possible sentences, and STAR). A CD contains all the reproducibles in the book, a bonus strategy, websites, and additional reproducibles.

Reading and Learning Strategies: Middle Grades through High School (Lenski, Wham, Johns, & Caskey, 2006) is another user-friendly book that contains approximately 140 strategies that focus on reading engagement, vocabulary, word study, comprehension, critical reading, studying, conducting research, and preparing for tests. The strategies are aimed at helping students learn more effectively in the content areas where informational (expository) text is often used. An included CD contains over 300 reproducibles and content area examples.

How Using the Spanish Reading Inventory Can Help Your Students

The results of the Spanish Reading Inventory can be used as a valuable basis for differentiated instruction. The insights can be used to inform instruction and prepare strategy lessons. The *total* results from the Spanish Reading Inventory must be used to help plan effective instructional interventions, taking into account each student's *specific* strengths and needs in word identification, comprehension, and/or fluency.

The Spanish Reading Inventory can provide data for:

- placing students in appropriate instructional materials,
- assessing reading behavior,
- providing helpful and appropriate interventions,
- differentiating instruction,
- developing reading strategy lessons, and
- helping students strengthen their reading.

CAUTION!

Unless the results are used in conjunction with daily instruction, observation, cumulative records, portfolios, and other evaluative techniques, serious errors may result. You should not underestimate the importance of the Spanish Reading Inventory for classroom, resource room, and clinical use; however, the results should be used to *guide* your responses to a student's reading. Results should not be used to dictate your actions, thereby dominating your professional knowledge and experience. Professionals who use the Spanish Reading Inventory as suggested in this manual will help ensure that students are placed in appropriate reading materials, taught needed reading strategies, and given appropriate interventions.

When you place students in reading materials at their appropriate instructional levels and provide responsive instructional interventions for specific areas of need, students will become better readers. That's the essence of realizing and acting upon "the point that individual differences are a fact of life in schools and classrooms" (Pearson, 2007, p. 155). Using the Spanish Reading Inventory to discover students' instructional levels and needs in reading, coupled with responsive teaching, is an appropriate way to design and implement high-quality reading instruction.

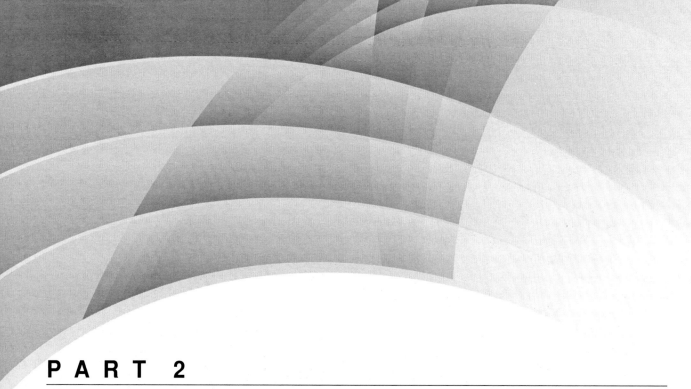

PART 2
Spanish Reading Inventory Forms and Performance Booklets

Graded Word Lists

Student Copy

List AA	**List A**
1. mi	1. abeja
2. papá	2. juego
3. sapo	3. silla
4. no	4. corre
5. él	5. hizo
6. vete	6. café
7. bebé	7. chivo
8. toma	8. lluvia
9. luna	9. queso
10. bonito	10. conejo
11. pelo	11. helado
12. todo	12. sobre
13. ala	13. encima
14. saluda	14. tenía
15. va	15. zapato
16. nido	16. cereza
17. amigo	17. ciudad
18. en	18. ayuda
19. rana	19. dueño
20. fue	20. guitarra

List A 7141

1. bruja
2. arreglar
3. programa
4. español
5. baile
6. terrible
7. trucha
8. pluma
9. bicicleta
10. invierno
11. gris
12. coyote
13. ladrillo
14. jaula
15. hoy
16. pueblito
17. alacrán
18. flecha
19. cumpleaños
20. cigüeña

List A 8224

1. granjero
2. oigan
3. píntamelo
4. alrededor
5. quiénes
6. pensamiento
7. demasiado
8. viuda
9. diccionario
10. juicio
11. cuadrado
12. bellísimo
13. dormilón
14. ausente
15. fuerte
16. mientras
17. puercoespín
18. hígado
19. tráigamela
20. ternura

List A 3183

1. ruiseñores
2. pingüino
3. caritativo
4. escabullirse
5. ordenado
6. crucero
7. perjudicial
8. encaminarse
9. contaminación
10. frambuesa
11. saxofón
12. pentágono
13. bayoneta
14. despiadado
15. desafortunado
16. impresionante
17. despistado
18. píquenmelas
19. comprémostelo
20. demuéstrenselo

Graded Passages
Student Copy

La Ranita Verde

Una ranita verde está sentada en una roca.
Sus patas de atrás son grandes y negras.

Salta muy bien.
Sabe nadar en la laguna.
Se moja.

Un Paseo en el Otoño

Era el otoño.

Elena salió a caminar.

Llevó a su perro Tito con ella.

A ellos les gusta caminar.

Ese día caminaron largo rato.

Vieron árboles.

Algunos tenían las hojas rojas.

Otros las tenían verdes.

Todos estaban bonitos.

Elena y Tito vieron unos pajaritos también.

Tito no les cayó atrás.

Se portó bien.

La Primera Nevada

Juan se despertó el sábado por la mañana. Miró el patio por la ventana. La tierra estaba blanca. Todos los árboles estaban blancos también.

"¡Ay, caramba!" comentó Juan.

"¿Qué dijiste?" le preguntó su hermano Tomás a medida que abría los ojos.

"¡Nevó anoche. Levántate y asómate por la ventana!"

Los dos muchachos corrieron a la ventana.

"¡Mira que linda la nieve!" dijo Tomás.

"Vamos a investigar cómo es. Vamos a vestirnos."

Juan y Tomás corrieron a la cocina.

"¡Mamá!" dijeron a la vez. "Nevó anoche."

"¡Sí!", les contestó la mamá. "Papá fue a comprarles unos trineos. Primero vamos a desayunar. Entonces pueden jugar en la nieve. Dicen que la primera nevada es la más bonita."

Duque Nada

Un día el dueño de Duque lo sacó a dar un paseo. El caliente sol brillaba. Duque caminó a la laguna. Allí vio una rana. La rana estaba posada en la rama de un árbol. Duque quería jugar con la rana. Empezó a ladrar. La rana saltó al agua. Entonces Duque saltó al agua. Pero no sabía qué hacer en el agua. El nivel del agua llegaba mucho más allá de su cabeza. Duque movió las patas. Pronto pudo sacar la cabeza del agua. Siguió pataleando. Al fin llegó al otro lado de la laguna. Así fue como aprendió a nadar.

Jorge está en las Montañas

Era la primera vez que Jorge iba camping con su familia. ¡Estaba tan contento de estar en las montañas! En cuanto prepararon la casa de campaña, él y su papá empezaron a explorar el área. Encontraron robles grandes, pinos gigantes, y muchas clases de flores.

De pronto notaron unas pequeñas huellas que parecían ser de animales. Vieron un ratón que se acercaba a un árbol y se metía en un pequeño agujero de éste. El ratón fue el único animal que vieron. Jorge sentía curiosidad por saber si todas las huellas eran las del ratoncito. Lo último que Jorge vio fue el nido de un pájaro en lo alto de un árbol.

El Oso Hambriento

Las hambrientas abejas se habían pasado el día entero haciendo miel. La noche estaba fresca y húmeda. Yo había dormido bien hasta oir un fuerte sonido cerca de la ventana. Pensé que alguien trataba de meterse en mi cabaña. Al acercarme pude ver algo negro al otro lado de la ventana. Del miedo salté y rompí el cristal de la ventana. Despacio y sin hacer ruido la figura negra caminó hacia atrás y desapareció.

El próximo día encontramos las huellas enormes de un oso. Parece que el oso había venido a buscar la miel que las abejas habían hecho y guardado en su panal.

El Incendio y los Animales

El verano había sido muy seco, algo raro para esta región del país. En el bosque, árboles, arbustos y flores se habían marchitado y quedado muertos. Este día la tranquilidad de la tarde fue interrumpida por una tormenta de truenos y relámpagos. Luego llovió largo rato.

Una chispa que saltó, prendió fuego a unas hojas secas. Las llamas se extendieron rapidamente. Los animales estuvieron ocupados advirtiéndose los unos a los otros del peligro a la vez que se esforzaban por escapar de las llamas.

Las ramas de los árboles estaban amarillas, anaranjadas y rojas. A medida que el fuego se acercaba los árboles se derrumbaban. El humo era tal que los animales no podían respirar. A muchos les fue imposible escapar de las llamas.

El Misterio

Todos dieron la vuelta y fijaron la vista en una figura con capa negra, que montada sobre una patineta, se deslizaba rápidamente a la vez que producía un gran silbido. Era un misterio porque nadie conocía a esta persona que patinaba tan bien.

José vio al patinador deslizarse por el pasamanos de la escalera de la biblioteca y desaparecer por el callejón. Al salir de la escuela Amelia siguió a la figura encapotada y observó la soltura con qué ésta saltó una curva y dio una vuelta en redondo. Luego, José vio una patineta y una chaqueta con capucha negra afuera de la casa de Rosa. También vio un libro de la biblioteca titulado *Cómo Hacer Piruetas en Patinetas* en el pupitre de ella. Entonces José supo que había resuelto el reto del misterio.

Mantén la Distancia

A Eduardo se le consideraba un muchacho difícil en el Colegio San Miguel. Todo el mundo lo llamaba Martín. Nadie se atrevía a pronunciar su verdadero nombre porque Martín se irritaba si lo hacían. No le gustaba su nombre. Era de un tamaño enorme y de lejos se parecía mucho al maestro Pérez. Apenas uno veía aparecer los zapatos y los pantalones de vaqueros descoloridos y rotos, se daba cuenta de que era Martín.

Tal vez era porque Martín se sentía inferior dado a la ropa que llevaba que se comportaba de una forma que asustaba e intimidaba a todo el mundo. El pobre no tenía muchos amigos excepto Raúl, un señor mayor que vivía en su edificio de apartamentos.

La Inminente Amenaza

Bajo el caliente sol del clima tropical las frentes de todo un grupo de hombres brillaban del sudor causado por el esfuerzo que hacían por caminar. Ellos eran guerrilleros que confiaban totalmente en el líder que creían sería la salvación de la patria.

Se habían propuesto llegar a una fortaleza bastante distante y planeaban atacar el almacén de la fortaleza con cohetes. Querían explotar la dinamita como si fuera una pequeña caja de fósforos encendidos.

Un hombre de tamaño impresionante dio una órden mientras que ellos mantenían la ardua marcha por la tierra deshabitada. Los guerrilleros pretendían que el ataque causara tal miedo en los soldados del fuerte que toda la población del pueblo de seguro quedaría convencida de la necesidad de unirse a la causa de la guerrilla.

La Búsqueda del Científico

Cristóbal, un científico, trabajaba muy concentrado en el laboratorio. Alguien le había mandado una carta con una sugerencia muy interesante. La clave del éxito de su descubrimiento estaba en la precisión de la reacción del elemento químico que activaría la medicina que él se esforzaba por formular. Desde ese momento era cuestión de ir reduciendo los diferentes componentes de la formula hasta identificar la cantidad necesaria para encontrar la fórmula ideal.

Al fin y al cabo él estaba seguro de que lo lograría. Entonces tendría en sus manos el monopolio de la medicina que haría posible la immortalidad del ser humano. ¡Cristóbal sería la única persona que sabría la proporción de los productos químicos en cada pastilla! El eliminar la muerte y todas las enfermedades conocidas convertiría a Cristóbal en la persona más poderosa en la tierra.

Performance Booklet

Teacher Copy

Second Edition

SPANISH READING INVENTORY PERFORMANCE BOOKLET

Jerry L. Johns, Ph.D. & Mayra C. Daniel, Ed.D.

Form A

Student _____ Grade _____ Sex M F Date of Test _____

School _____ Examiner _____ Date of Birth _____

Address _____ Current Book/Level_____ Age_____

SUMMARY OF STUDENT'S READING PERFORMANCE

Grade	Word Recognition						Comprehension		Reading Rate	
	Isolation (Word Lists)				Context (Passages)		Form A		Words per Minute (WPM)	Norm Group Per-centile
	Sight	Anal-ysis	Total	Level	Mis-cues	Level	Ques-tions Missed	Level		
PP1	■	■	■	■						
PP2										
P										
1										
2										
3										
4	■	■	■	■						
5	■	■	■	■						
6	■	■	■	■						
7	■	■	■	■						
8	■	■	■	■						

ESTIMATE OF READING LEVELS: Independent _____ Instructional _____ Frustration _____

LISTENING LEVEL

Grade	Form _____	
	Questions Missed	Level
1		
2		
3		
4		
5		
6		
7		
8		

ESTIMATED LEVEL: _____

GENERAL OBSERVATIONS

INFORMAL ANALYSIS OF ORAL READING

Oral Reading Behaviors	Frequency of Occurrence			General Impact on Meaning		
	Seldom	Sometimes	Frequently	No Change	Little Change	Much Change
Substitutions						
Insertions						
Omissions						
Reversals						
Repetitions						

QUALITATIVE ANALYSIS OF SPANISH READING INVENTORY INSIGHTS

General Directions: Note the degree to which the student shows behavior or evidence in the following areas. Space is provided for additional items.

	Seldom Weak Poor			Always Strong Excellent

COMPREHENSION

Seeks to construct meaning
Makes predictions
Activates background knowledge
Possesses appropriate concepts and vocabulary
Monitors reading
Varies reading rate as needed
Understands topic and major ideas
Remembers facts or details
Makes and supports appropriate inferences
Evaluates ideas from passages
Understands vocabulary used
Provides appropriate definitions of words
Engages with passages

_____
_____

WORD IDENTIFICATION

Possesses numerous strategies
Uses strategies flexibly
Uses graphophonic information
Uses semantic information
Uses syntactic information
Knows basic sight words automatically
Possesses sight vocabulary

_____
_____

ORAL AND SILENT READING

Reads fluently
Reads with expression
Attends to punctuation
Keeps place while reading
Reads at appropriate rate
Reads silently without vocalization

_____
_____

ATTITUDE AND CONFIDENCE

Enjoys reading
Demonstrates willingness to risk
Possesses positive self-concept
Chooses to read
Regards himself/herself as a reader
Exhibits persistence

_____
_____

Form A • Graded Word Lists • Performance Booklet • Student Copy is on page 54.

List AA (Pre-Primer)	Sight	Analysis	List A (Primer)	Sight	Analysis
1. mi	_____	_____	1. abeja	_____	_____
2. papá	_____	_____	2. juego	_____	_____
3. sapo	_____	_____	3. silla	_____	_____
4. no	_____	_____	4. corre	_____	_____
5. él	_____	_____	5. hizo	_____	_____
6. vete	_____	_____	6. café	_____	_____
7. bebé	_____	_____	7. chivo	_____	_____
8. toma	_____	_____	8. lluvia	_____	_____
9. luna	_____	_____	9. queso	_____	_____
10. bonito	_____	_____	10. conejo	_____	_____
11. pelo	_____	_____	11. helado	_____	_____
12. todo	_____	_____	12. sobre	_____	_____
13. ala	_____	_____	13. encima	_____	_____
14. saluda	_____	_____	14. tenía	_____	_____
15. va	_____	_____	15. zapato	_____	_____
16. nido	_____	_____	16. cereza	_____	_____
17. amigo	_____	_____	17. ciudad	_____	_____
18. en	_____	_____	18. ayuda	_____	_____
19. rana	_____	_____	19. dueño	_____	_____
20. fue	_____	_____	20. guitarra	_____	_____
Number Correct	_____	_____	Number Correct	_____	_____
Total	_____		Total	_____	

Scoring Guide for Graded Word Lists			
Independent	Instructional	Inst./Frust.	Frustration
20 19	18 17 16	15 14	13 or less

From Jerry L. Johns and Mayra C. Daniel, *Spanish Reading Inventory: Pre-Primer through Grade Eight* (2nd ed.). Copyright © 2010 by Kendall Hunt Publishing Company (1-800-247-3458). May be reproduced for noncommercial educational purposes. Website: www.kendallhunt.com

Form A • Graded Word Lists • Performance Booklet • Student Copy is on page 55.

List A 7141 (Grade 1)	Sight	Analysis	List A 8224 (Grade 2)	Sight	Analysis
1. bruja	_____	_____	1. granjero	_____	_____
2. arreglar	_____	_____	2. oigan	_____	_____
3. programa	_____	_____	3. píntamelo	_____	_____
4. español	_____	_____	4. alrededor	_____	_____
5. baile	_____	_____	5. quiénes	_____	_____
6. terrible	_____	_____	6. pensamiento	_____	_____
7. trucha	_____	_____	7. demasiado	_____	_____
8. pluma	_____	_____	8. viuda	_____	_____
9. bicicleta	_____	_____	9. diccionario	_____	_____
10. invierno	_____	_____	10. juicio	_____	_____
11. gris	_____	_____	11. cuadrado	_____	_____
12. coyote	_____	_____	12. bellísimo	_____	_____
13. ladrillo	_____	_____	13. dormilón	_____	_____
14. jaula	_____	_____	14. ausente	_____	_____
15. hoy	_____	_____	15. fuerte	_____	_____
16. pueblito	_____	_____	16. mientras	_____	_____
17. alacrán	_____	_____	17. puercoespín	_____	_____
18. flecha	_____	_____	18. hígado	_____	_____
19. cumpleaños	_____	_____	19. tráigamela	_____	_____
20. cigüeña	_____	_____	20. ternura	_____	_____
Number Correct	_____	_____	Number Correct	_____	_____
Total	_____		Total	_____	

Scoring Guide for Graded Word Lists			
Independent	Instructional	Inst./Frust.	Frustration
20 19	18 17 16	15 14	13 or less

Form A • Graded Word List • Performance Booklet • Student Copy is on page 56.

List A 3183　　　　**Sight**　　　　**Analysis**
(Grade 3)

1. ruiseñores _____ _____

2. pingüino _____ _____

3. caritativo _____ _____

4. escabullirse _____ _____

5. ordenado _____ _____

6. crucero _____ _____

7. perjudicial _____ _____

8. encaminarse _____ _____

9. contaminación _____ _____

10. frambuesa _____ _____

11. saxofón _____ _____

12. pentágono _____ _____

13. bayoneta _____ _____

14. despiadado _____ _____

15. desafortunado _____ _____

16. impresionante _____ _____

17. despistado _____ _____

18. píquenmelas _____ _____

19. comprémostelo _____ _____

20. demuéstrenselo _____ _____

Number Correct _____ _____

Total _____

Scoring Guide for Graded Word Lists			
Independent	Instructional	Inst./Frust.	Frustration
20 19	18 17 16	15 14	13 or less

From Jerry L. Johns and Mayra C. Daniel, *Spanish Reading Inventory: Pre-Primer through Grade Eight* (2nd ed.). Copyright © 2010 by Kendall Hunt Publishing Company (1-800-247-3458). May be reproduced for noncommercial educational purposes. Website: www.kendallhunt.com

Student Copy is on page 58.

AAA (Pre-Primer 1) Activating Background: Lee el título a ti mismo. Luego dime qué crees que va a pasar en el cuento.

Background: Low ├──────┼──────┤ High

La Ranita Verde

		MISCUES						
	Substitution	Insertion	Omission	Reversal	Repetition	Self-Correction of Unacceptable Miscue	Meaning Change (Significant Miscue)	
Una ranita verde está sentada en una roca. 8								
Sus patas de atrás son grandes y negras. 16								
Salta muy bien. 19								
Sabe nadar en la laguna. 24								
Se moja. 26								
TOTAL								

Total Miscues ☐   Significant Miscues ☐

Word Recognition Scoring Guide		
Total Miscues	Level	Significant Miscues
0	Independent	0
1	Ind./Inst.	–
2	Instructional	1
3	Inst./Frust.	2
4 +	Frustration	3 +

Oral Reading Rate	Norm Group Percentile
$\overline{)1560}$ WPM	☐ 90 ☐ 75 ☐ 50 ☐ 25 ☐ 10

From Jerry L. Johns and Mayra C. Daniel, *Spanish Reading Inventory: Pre-Primer through Grade Eight* (2nd ed.). Copyright © 2010 by Kendall Hunt Publishing Company (1-800-247-3458). May be reproduced for noncommercial educational purposes. Website: www.kendallhunt.com

AAA (Pre-Primer 1)
Comprehension Questions

F   1. _____   ¿Dónde está sentada la ranita?
                    (en una roca)

F   2. _____   ¿Dónde nada?
                    (en una laguna)

E   3. _____   ¿Qué les gusta hacer a las ranas?
                    (saltar, nadar)

I   4. _____   ¿Por qué será que las ranas saltan
                    tan alto?
                    (cualquier respuesta lógica)

V   5. _____   ¿Qué es *una rana*?
                    (un animal; un animal que salta)

Retelling/Notes

☐ Questions Missed

Comprehension Scoring Guide	
Questions Missed	Level
0	Independent
1	Ind./Inst.
1½	Instructional
2	Inst./Frust.
2½ +	Frustration

Retelling
Excellent
Satisfactory
Unsatisfactory

From Jerry L. Johns and Mayra C. Daniel, *Spanish Reading Inventory: Pre-Primer through Grade Eight* (2nd ed.). Copyright © 2010 by Kendall Hunt Publishing Company (1-800-247-3458). May be reproduced for noncommercial educational purposes. Website: www.kendallhunt.com

Student Copy is on page 59.

AA (Pre-Primer 2) Activating Background: Lee el título a ti mismo. Luego dime qué crees que va a pasar en el cuento.

Background: Low ├──────┼──────┤ High

Un Paseo en el Otoño			MISCUES						
		Substitution	Insertion	Omission	Reversal	Repetition	Self-Correction of Unacceptable Miscue	Meaning Change (Significant Miscue)	
Era el otoño.	3								
Elena salió a caminar.	7								
Llevó a su perro Tito con ella.	14								
A ellos les gusta caminar.	19								
Ese día caminaron largo rato.	24								
Vieron árboles.	26								
Algunos tenían las hojas rojas.	31								
Otros las tenían verdes.	35								
Todos estaban bonitos.	38								
Elena y Tito vieron unos pajaritos también.	45								
Tito no les cayó atrás.	50								
Se portó bien.	53								
TOTAL									

Total Miscues ☐   Significant Miscues ☐

Word Recognition Scoring Guide		
Total Miscues	Level	Significant Miscues
0	Independent	0
1–2	Ind./Inst.	1
3	Instructional	2
4	Inst./Frust.	3
5 +	Frustration	4 +

Oral Reading Rate	Norm Group Percentile
⎯⎯ WPM)3180	☐ 90 ☐ 75 ☐ 50 ☐ 25 ☐ 10

AA (Pre-Primer 2)
Comprehension Questions

F 1. _____   Según el cuento, ¿qué estación del año es?
                  (otoño)

F 2. _____   ¿Qué salió a hacer Elena?
                  (salió a caminar)

E 3. _____   ¿Por qué crees que Elena se llevó a su perro con ella?
                  (lo quiere; no quiere salir sola; cualquier respuesta lógica)

I 4. _____   ¿Por qué crees que Tito no les cayó atrás a los pajaritos?
                  (cualquier respuesta lógica)

V 5. _____   ¿Qué quiere decir la palabra *bonitos*?
                  (lindos; de colores; cualquier respuesta lógica)

Retelling/Notes

▢ Questions Missed

Comprehension Scoring Guide	
Questions Missed	Level
0	Independent
1	Ind./Inst.
1½	Instructional
2	Inst./Frust.
2½ +	Frustration

Retelling
Excellent
Satisfactory
Unsatisfactory

Student Copy is on page 60.

A (Primer) Activating Background: Lee el título a ti mismo. Luego dime qué crees que va a pasar en el cuento.

Background: Low ├──────┼──────┤ High

La Primera Nevada		MISCUES						
		Substitution	Insertion	Omission	Reversal	Repetition	Self-Correction of Unacceptable Miscue	Meaning Change (Significant Miscue)
Juan se despertó el sábado por la mañana.	8							
Miró el patio por la ventana. La tierra estaba	17							
blanca. Todos los árboles estaban blancos	23							
también.	24							
"¡Ay, caramba!" comentó Juan.	28							
"¿Qué dijiste?" le preguntó su hermano	34							
Tomás a medida que abría los ojos.	41							
"¡Nevó anoche. Levántate y asómate por la	48							
ventana!"	49							
Los dos muchachos corrieron a la ventana.	56							
"¡Mira que linda la nieve!" dijo Tomás.	63							
"Vamos a investigar cómo es. Vamos a	70							
vestirnos."	71							
Juan y Tomás corrieron a la cocina.	78							
"¡Mamá!" dijeron a la vez. "Nevó anoche."	85							
"¡Sí!", les contestó la mamá. "Papá fue a	93							
comprarles unos trineos. Primero vamos a	99							
desayunar. Entonces pueden jugar en la nieve.	106							
Dicen que la primera nevada es la más bonita."	115							
TOTAL								

Total Miscues ☐ **Significant Miscues** ☐

Word Recognition Scoring Guide		
Total Miscues	Level	Significant Miscues
0–2	Independent	0–1
3–5	Ind./Inst.	2
6	Instructional	3
7–11	Inst./Frust.	4–5
12 +	Frustration	6 +

Oral Reading Rate	Norm Group Percentile
⟍6900 WPM	☐ 90 ☐ 75 ☐ 50 ☐ 25 ☐ 10

From Jerry L. Johns and Mayra C. Daniel, *Spanish Reading Inventory: Pre-Primer through Grade Eight* (2nd ed.). Copyright © 2010 by Kendall Hunt Publishing Company (1-800-247-3458). May be reproduced for noncommercial educational purposes. Website: www.kendallhunt.com

A (Primer)
Comprehension Questions

Retelling/Notes

T   1. _____ ¿De qué se trata el cuento?
(de dos niños; de la nieve; de dos niños que juegan en la nieve)

F   2. _____ ¿Qué día ocurre el cuento?
(el sábado)

F   3. _____ ¿Qué vieron los niños cuando despertaron?
(que había nevado; que los árboles estaban blancos)

F   4. _____ ¿Quién se despertó primero?
(Juan)

F   5. _____ ¿Qué fue a hacer el papá de Juan y Tomás?
(fue a comprarles unos trineos a sus hijos)

F   6. _____ ¿Cómo se veían los árboles?
(blancos; cubiertos de nieve)

I   7. _____ ¿Por qué crees que los niños se pusieron tan contentos?
(cualquier respuesta lógica; querían jugar en la nieve)

I   8. _____ ¿Por qué crees que Juan y Tomás no salieron en seguida?
(cualquier respuesta lógica; la mamá les dijo que primero tenían que vestirse y desayunar; la mamá les dijo que esperaran)

E   9. _____ ¿Qué crees que la familia iba a hacer con la nieve?
(cualquier respuesta lógica; tocar la nieve; probar la nieve; hacer bolas con la nieve y tirarlas)

V   10. _____ ¿Qué crees que es *un trineo*?
(algo que se monta; algo que se usa en la nieve; cualquier respuesta lógica)

☐ Questions Missed

Comprehension Scoring Guide	
Questions Missed	Level
0–1	Independent
1½–2	Ind./Inst.
2½	Instructional
3–4½	Inst./Frust.
5 +	Frustration

Retelling
Excellent
Satisfactory
Unsatisfactory

From Jerry L. Johns and Mayra C. Daniel, *Spanish Reading Inventory: Pre-Primer through Grade Eight* (2nd ed.). Copyright © 2010 by Kendall Hunt Publishing Company (1-800-247-3458). May be reproduced for noncommercial educational purposes. Website: www.kendallhunt.com

Student Copy is on page 61.

A 7141 (Grade 1) Activating Background: Lee el título a ti mismo. Luego dime qué crees que va a pasar en el cuento.

Background: Low |————+————| High

Duque Nada

		Substitution	Insertion	Omission	Reversal	Repetition	Self-Correction of Unacceptable Miscue	Meaning Change (Significant Miscue)
		MISCUES						
Un día el dueño de Duque lo sacó a dar un	11							
paseo. El caliente sol brillaba. Duque caminó a	19							
la laguna. Allí vio una rana. La rana estaba	28							
posada en la rama de un árbol. Duque quería	37							
jugar con la rana. Empezó a ladrar. La rana	46							
saltó al agua. Entonces Duque saltó al agua.	54							
Pero no sabía qué hacer en el agua. El nivel del	65							
agua llegaba mucho más allá de su cabeza.	73							
Duque movió las patas. Pronto pudo sacar la	81							
cabeza del agua. Siguió pataleando. Al fin llegó	89							
al otro lado de la laguna. Así fue como aprendió	99							
a nadar.	101							
TOTAL								

Total Miscues [ ]   Significant Miscues [ ]

Word Recognition Scoring Guide		
Total Miscues	Level	Significant Miscues
0–1	Independent	0–1
2–4	Ind./Inst.	2
5	Instructional	3
6–9	Inst./Frust.	4
10 +	Frustration	5 +

Oral Reading Rate	Norm Group Percentile
⎯⎯ WPM)6060	☐ 90 ☐ 75 ☐ 50 ☐ 25 ☐ 10

A 7141 (Grade 1)
Comprehension Questions

<table>
<tr><td>T</td><td>1. _____</td><td>¿De qué se trata el cuento?
(de una rana; de un perro; de como
Duque aprendió a nadar)</td></tr>
<tr><td>F</td><td>2. _____</td><td>¿Adónde fue Duque?
(a una laguna)</td></tr>
<tr><td>F</td><td>3. _____</td><td>¿Qué vio Duque?
(el sol brillante; una rana)</td></tr>
<tr><td>F</td><td>4. _____</td><td>¿Qué pasó cuando Duque vio la
rana?
(ladró; saltó al agua; movió las
patas; sacó la cabeza del agua;
pataleó; aprendió a nadar)</td></tr>
<tr><td>F</td><td>5. _____</td><td>¿Qué hizo Duque cuando el agua le
cubrió la cabeza?
(movió las patas, no sabía qué
hacer; cualquier respuesta lógica)</td></tr>
<tr><td>F</td><td>6. _____</td><td>¿Qué aprendió Duque en este
cuento?
(aprendió a nadar)</td></tr>
<tr><td>I</td><td>7. _____</td><td>¿Por qué crees que la rana saltó al
agua?
(cualquier respuesta lógica; para
nadar; para escaparse de Duque)</td></tr>
<tr><td>I</td><td>8. _____</td><td>¿Quién era Duque?
(un perro)</td></tr>
<tr><td>E</td><td>9. _____</td><td>¿Por qué crees que Duque quería
jugar con la rana?
(cualquier respuesta lógica; por
curiosidad; para poder jugar con
otro animal)</td></tr>
<tr><td>V</td><td>10. _____</td><td>¿Qué es una laguna?
(un lugar con agua; es para nadar;
cualquier respuesta lógica)</td></tr>
</table>

Retelling/Notes

[ ] Questions Missed

Comprehension Scoring Guide	
Questions Missed	Level
0–1	Independent
1½–2	Ind./Inst.
2½	Instructional
3–4½	Inst./Frust.
5 +	Frustration

Retelling
Excellent
Satisfactory
Unsatisfactory

Student Copy is on page 62.

A 8224 (Grade 2) Activating Background: Lee el título a ti mismo. Luego dime qué crees que va a pasar en el cuento.

Background: Low |——+——| High

Jorge está en las Montañas		Substitution	Insertion	Omission	Reversal	Repetition	Self-Correction of Unacceptable Miscue	Meaning Change (Significant Miscue)
		MISCUES						
Era la primera vez que Jorge iba camping con	9							
su familia. ¡Estaba tan contento de estar en las	18							
montañas! En cuanto prepararon la casa de	25							
campaña, él y su papá empezaron a explorar el	34							
área. Encontraron robles grandes, pinos	39							
gigantes, y muchas clases de flores.	45							
De pronto notaron unas pequeñas huellas que	52							
parecían ser de animales. Vieron un ratón que	60							
se acercaba a un árbol y se metía en un pequeño	71							
agujero de éste. El ratón fue el único animal que	81							
vieron. Jorge sentía curiosidad por saber si todas	89							
las huellas eran las del ratoncito. Lo último que	98							
Jorge vio fue el nido de un pájaro en lo alto de	110							
un árbol.	112							
TOTAL								

Total Miscues ☐ **Significant Miscues** ☐

Word Recognition Scoring Guide		
Total Miscues	Level	Significant Miscues
0–1	Independent	0–1
2–4	Ind./Inst.	2
5	Instructional	3
6–11	Inst./Frust.	4–5
12 +	Frustration	6 +

Oral Reading Rate	Norm Group Percentile
)6720 WPM	☐ 90 ☐ 75 ☐ 50 ☐ 25 ☐ 10

From Jerry L. Johns and Mayra C. Daniel, *Spanish Reading Inventory: Pre-Primer through Grade Eight* (2nd ed.). Copyright © 2010 by Kendall Hunt Publishing Company (1-800-247-3458). May be reproduced for noncommercial educational purposes. Website: www.kendallhunt.com

Comprehension Questions

T   1. _____ ¿De qué se trata el cuento?
(de un muchacho que va camping
con su familia)

F   2. _____ ¿Le gustó a Jorge ir camping con
su familia? ¿Cómo sabes?
(le gustó; se puso contento)

F   3. _____ ¿Por qué dieron un paseo Jorge y
su papá?
(para explorar el área)

F   4. _____ ¿Qué clase de árboles encontraron?
(pinos; robles)

F   5. _____ Además del ratón, ¿qué vio Jorge?
(huellas de animales; el nido de un
pájaro)

F   6. _____ ¿Dónde se metió el ratón?
(en un agujero)

I   7. _____ ¿Por qué crees que el ratón se
metió en el agujero?
(cualquier respuesta lógica; quiso
esconderse; oyó a Jorge y sintió
miedo)

I   8. _____ ¿Por qué crees que Jorge y su papá
pensaron que las huellas eran de
animales?
(cualquier respuesta lógica)

E   9. _____ ¿Qué otros animales crees que
Jorge podría encontrar si diera otro
paseo?
(cualquier respuesta lógica)

V   10. _____ ¿Qué son *huellas*?
(donde se para un animal; marcas
en la tierra; cualquier respuesta
lógica)

Retelling/Notes

[ ] Questions Missed

Comprehension Scoring Guide	
Questions Missed	Level
0–1	Independent
1½–2	Ind./Inst.
2½	Instructional
3–4½	Inst./Frust.
5 +	Frustration

Retelling
Excellent
Satisfactory
Unsatisfactory

Student Copy is on page 63.

A 3183 (Grade 3) Activating Background: Lee el título a ti mismo. Luego dime qué crees que va a pasar en el cuento.

Background: Low ├────────┼────────┤ High

El Oso Hambriento		MISCUES						
		Substitution	Insertion	Omission	Reversal	Repetition	Self-Correction of Unacceptable Miscue	Meaning Change (Significant Miscue)
Las hambrientas abejas se habían pasado el	7							
día entero haciendo miel. La noche estaba fresca	15							
y húmeda. Yo había dormido bien hasta oir un	24							
fuerte sonido cerca de la ventana. Pensé que	32							
alguien trataba de meterse en mi cabaña. Al	40							
acercarme pude ver algo negro al otro lado de la	50							
ventana. Del miedo salté y rompí el cristal de la	60							
ventana. Despacio y sin hacer ruido la figura	68							
negra caminó hacia atrás y desapareció.	74							
El próximo día encontramos las huellas	80							
enormes de un oso. Parece que el oso había	89							
venido a buscar la miel que las abejas habían	98							
hecho y guardado en su panal.	104							
TOTAL								

Total Miscues ☐   Significant Miscues ☐

Word Recognition Scoring Guide		
Total Miscues	Level	Significant Miscues
0–1	Independent	0–1
2–4	Ind./Inst.	2
5	Instructional	3
6–9	Inst./Frust.	4
10 +	Frustration	5 +

Oral Reading Rate	Norm Group Percentile
⎯⎯⎯ WPM ⟌6240	☐ 90 ☐ 75 ☐ 50 ☐ 25 ☐ 10

A 3183 (Grade 3)
Comprehension Questions

T 1. _____ ¿De qué se trata este cuento?
(de un oso que buscaba miel; del
susto que tuvo una persona; del
miedo que tuvo una persona)

F 2. _____ ¿Por qué se despertó la persona?
(oyó un ruido; pensó que alguien se
metía en la cabaña)

F 3. _____ ¿Qué habían hecho las abejas todo
el día?
(miel)

F 4. _____ ¿Dónde guardaron la miel las
abejas?
(en el panal)

F 5. _____ ¿Qué vio la persona cerca de la
ventana?
(una figura negra)

F 6. _____ ¿Qué encontraron al día siguiente?
(las huellas de un oso)

F 7. _____ ¿Cómo crees que se sintió la
persona el día siguiente? ¿Por qué?
(cualquier respuesta lógica;
asustada, sorprendida)

I 8. _____ ¿Por qué crees que el oso se fue?
(cualquier respuesta lógica; vio
la sombra de la persona; no pudo
entrar a la cabaña)

E 9. _____ ¿Qué harías tú para que el oso no
regresara?
(cualquier respuesta lógica; quitar el
panal; cambiar el lugar del panal)

V 10. _____ ¿Qué es *un panal*?
(donde está la miel; donde las abejas
guardan su miel; cualquier respuesta
lógica)

Retelling/Notes

☐ Questions Missed

Comprehension Scoring Guide	
Questions Missed	Level
0–1	Independent
1½–2	Ind./Inst.
2½	Instructional
3–4½	Inst./Frust.
5 +	Frustration

Retelling
Excellent
Satisfactory
Unsatisfactory

From Jerry L. Johns and Mayra C. Daniel, *Spanish Reading Inventory: Pre-Primer through Grade Eight* (2nd ed.). Copyright © 2010 by Kendall Hunt Publishing Company (1-800-247-3458). May be reproduced for noncommercial educational purposes. Website: www.kendallhunt.com

Student Copy is on page 64.

A 5414 (Grade 4) Activating Background: Lee el título a ti mismo. Luego dime qué crees que va a pasar en el cuento.

Background: Low ├──────┼──────┤ High

El Incendio y los Animales

		Substitution	Insertion	Omission	Reversal	Repetition	Self-Correction of Unacceptable Miscue	Meaning Change (Significant Miscue)
El verano había sido muy seco, algo raro para	9							
esta región del país. En el bosque, árboles,	17							
arbustos y flores se habían marchitado y quedado	25							
muertos. Este día la tranquilidad de la tarde fue	34							
interrumpida por una tormenta de truenos y	41							
relámpagos. Luego llovió largo rato.	46							
Una chispa que saltó, prendió fuego a unas	54							
hojas secas. Las llamas se extendieron	60							
rapidamente. Los animales estuvieron ocupados	65							
advirtiéndose los unos a los otros del peligro a la	75							
vez que se esforzaban por escapar de las llamas.	84							
Las ramas de los árboles estaban amarillas,	91							
anaranjadas y rojas. A medida que el fuego se	100							
acercaba los árboles se derrumbaban. El humo	107							
era tal que los animales no podían respirar. A	116							
muchos les fue imposible escapar de las llamas.	124							
TOTAL								

MISCUES

Total Miscues ☐   Significant Miscues ☐

Word Recognition Scoring Guide		
Total Miscues	Level	Significant Miscues
0–2	Independent	0–1
3–5	Ind./Inst.	2
6	Instructional	3
7–12	Inst./Frust.	4–5
13 +	Frustration	6 +

Oral Reading Rate	Norm Group Percentile
⎯⎯⎯ WPM)7440	☐ 90 ☐ 75 ☐ 50 ☐ 25 ☐ 10

Comprehension Questions

| | | Retelling/Notes |

T   1. _____ ¿De qué se trata la historia?
(de un fuego; de un incendio)

F   2. _____ ¿Qué trataron de hacer los animales?
(ayudarse los unos a los otros;
advertirse los unos a los otros del
peligro; escaparse; salvarse; huir)

F   3. _____ ¿Cómo había sido diferente el
verano?
(había sido muy seco; había estado
raro)

F   4. _____ ¿Cómo fue interrumpida la
tranquilidad de la tarde?
(una tormenta; truenos y
relámpagos; llovió largo rato)

F   5. _____ ¿De qué colores estaban las ramas
de los árboles mientras que se
quemaban?
(amarillas, rojas, y anaranjadas)

F   6. _____ ¿Por qué no podían respirar los
animales?
(había mucho humo)

I   7. _____ ¿Por qué crees que el incendio se
extendió rápidamente?
(cualquier respuesta lógica; el
verano había estado muy seco)

I   8. _____ ¿Qué puede haber causado el fuego?
(un relámpago; un trueno)

E   9. _____ ¿Qué problemas podrían tener los
animales que sobrevivieron?
(cualquier respuesta lógica)

V   10. _____ ¿Qué significa la palabra *escaparse*?
(irse; salir de un peligro; cualquier
respuesta lógica)

Retelling/Notes

| | Questions Missed |

Comprehension Scoring Guide	
Questions Missed	Level
0–1	Independent
1½–2	Ind./Inst.
2½	Instructional
3–4½	Inst./Frust.
5 +	Frustration

Retelling
Excellent
Satisfactory
Unsatisfactory

Student Copy is on page 65.

A 8595 (Grade 5) Activating Background: Lee el título a ti mismo. Luego dime qué crees que va a pasar en el cuento.

Background: Low |———|———| High

El Misterio		Substitution	Insertion	Omission	Reversal	Repetition	Self-Correction of Unacceptable Miscue	Meaning Change (Significant Miscue)
		MISCUES						
Todos dieron la vuelta y fijaron la vista en una	10							
figura con capa negra, que montada sobre una	18							
patineta, se deslizaba rápidamente a la vez que	26							
producía un gran silbido. Era un misterio	33							
porque nadie conocía a esta persona que	40							
patinaba tan bien.	43							
José vio al patinador deslizarse por el	50							
pasamanos de la escalera de la biblioteca y	58							
desaparecer por el callejón. Al salir de la	66							
escuela Amelia siguió a la figura encapotada y	74							
observó la soltura con qué ésta saltó una curva y	84							
dio una vuelta en redondo. Luego, José vio una	93							
patineta y una chaqueta con capucha negra	100							
afuera de la casa de Rosa. También vio un libro	110							
de la biblioteca titulado *Cómo Hacer Piruetas en*	118							
Patinetas en el pupitre de ella. Entonces José	126							
supo que había resuelto el reto del misterio.	134							
TOTAL								

Word Recognition Scoring Guide		
Total Miscues	Level	Significant Miscues
0–2	Independent	0–1
3–5	Ind./Inst.	2
6	Instructional	3
7–12	Inst./Frust.	4–5
13 +	Frustration	6 +

Total Miscues [ ]   **Significant Miscues** [ ]

Oral Reading Rate	Norm Group Percentile
WPM)8040	☐ 90 ☐ 75 ☐ 50 ☐ 25 ☐ 10

A 8595 (Grade 5)
Comprehension Questions

T   1. _____ ¿De qué se trata este cuento?
(de alguien que patinaba; de una
figura misteriosa)

F   2. _____ ¿Cómo vestía la figura misteriosa?
(con capa negra; con una capucha
negra)

F   3. _____ ¿Por qué era la persona del cuento
un misterio?
(nadie sabía quién era; cualquier
respuesta lógica)

F   4. _____ ¿Quién vio a la figura en patineta?
(José; todos; Amelia)

F   5. _____ ¿Qué tipo de trucos hizo la figura
de capa negra?
(se deslizó por el pasamanos de
la escalera; se desapareció por el
callejón)

F   6. _____ ¿Quién resolvió el misterio?
(José)

F   7. _____ ¿Qué vio José que le ayudó a
resolver el misterio?
(la patineta; la chaqueta de capucha
negra; el libro)

I   8. _____ En fin, ¿quién era la persona
misteriosa?
(Rosa)

E   9. _____ Si tú fueras José, ¿de qué otra
forma crees que podrías haber
resuelto el misterio?
(cualquier respuesta lógica)

V 10. _____ ¿Qué significa la palabra
deslizarse?
(bajarse; resbalarse; cualquier
respuesta lógica)

Retelling/Notes

☐ Questions Missed

Comprehension Scoring Guide	
Questions Missed	Level
0–1	Independent
1½–2	Ind./Inst.
2½	Instructional
3–4½	Inst./Frust.
5 +	Frustration

Retelling
Excellent
Satisfactory
Unsatisfactory

From Jerry L. Johns and Mayra C. Daniel, *Spanish Reading Inventory: Pre-Primer through Grade Eight* (2nd ed.). Copyright © 2010 by Kendall Hunt Publishing Company (1-800-247-3458). May be reproduced for noncommercial educational purposes. Website: www.kendallhunt.com

Student Copy is on page 66.

A 6867 (Grade 6) Activating Background: Lee el título a ti mismo. Luego dime qué crees que va a pasar en el cuento.

Background: Low ├────┼────┤ High

Mantén la Distancia

	Substitution	Insertion	Omission	Reversal	Repetition	Self-Correction of Unacceptable Miscue	Meaning Change (Significant Miscue)
A Eduardo se le consideraba un muchacho 7							
difícil en el Colegio San Miguel. Todo el 15							
mundo lo llamaba Martín. Nadie se atrevía a 23							
pronunciar su verdadero nombre porque Martín 29							
se irritaba si lo hacían. No le gustaba su 38							
nombre. Era de un tamaño enorme y de lejos se 48							
parecía mucho al maestro Pérez. Apenas uno 55							
veía aparecer los zapatos y los pantalones de 63							
vaqueros descoloridos y rotos, se daba cuenta de 71							
que era Martín. 74							
Tal vez era porque Martín se sentía inferior 82							
dado a la ropa que llevaba que se comportaba de 92							
una forma que asustaba e intimidaba a todo el 101							
mundo. El pobre no tenía muchos amigos 108							
excepto Raúl, un señor mayor que vivía en su 117							
edificio de apartamentos. 120							
TOTAL							

Total Miscues [ ]   Significant Miscues [ ]

Word Recognition Scoring Guide		
Total Miscues	Level	Significant Miscues
0–2	Independent	0–1
3–5	Ind./Inst.	2
6	Instructional	3
7–12	Inst./Frust.	4–5
13 +	Frustration	6 +

Oral Reading Rate	Norm Group Percentile
⎯⎯⎯ WPM)7200	☐ 90 ☐ 75 ☐ 50 ☐ 25 ☐ 10

From Jerry L. Johns and Mayra C. Daniel, *Spanish Reading Inventory: Pre-Primer through Grade Eight* (2nd ed.). Copyright © 2010 by Kendall Hunt Publishing Company (1-800-247-3458). May be reproduced for noncommercial educational purposes. Website: www.kendallhunt.com

A **6867** (Grade 6)
Comprehension Questions

T   1. _____ ¿De qué se trata este cuento?
(un muchacho que se llama
Eduardo)

F   2. _____ ¿Cómo consideraba todo el
mundo a Eduardo?
(un muchacho difícil)

F   3. _____ ¿A qué escuela asistía Eduardo?
(al Colegio San Miguel)

F   4. _____ ¿Cómo era/ Qué tipo tenía
Eduardo?
(un tamaño enorme; se parecía al
maestro Pérez)

F   5. _____ ¿Qué ropas llevaba Eduardo?
(pantalones de vaqueros
descoloridos y rotos)

F   6. _____ ¿Qué nombre le llamaba todo el
mundo a Eduardo?
(Martín)

F   7. _____ ¿Cómo se comportaba Eduardo?
(asustaba a la gente; intimidaba a
la gente)

I   8. _____ ¿Por qué sería Raúl su amigo?
(cualquier respuesta lógica; vivía
en el mismo edificio; le tenía
lástima)

E   9. _____ ¿Serías tú amigo de Eduardo si
asistieras al Colegio San Miguel?
(cualquier respuesta lógica)

V 10. _____ ¿Qué significa la palabra
intimidar?
(darle miedo a alguien; hacer
sentir mal a otra persona;
cualquier respuesta lógica)

Retelling/Notes

[ ] Questions Missed

Comprehension Scoring Guide	
Questions Missed	Level
0–1	Independent
1½–2	Ind./Inst.
2½	Instructional
3–4½	Inst./Frust.
5 +	Frustration

Retelling
Excellent
Satisfactory
Unsatisfactory

From Jerry L. Johns and Mayra C. Daniel, *Spanish Reading Inventory: Pre-Primer through Grade Eight* (2nd ed.). Copyright © 2010 by Kendall Hunt Publishing Company (1-800-247-3458). May be reproduced for noncommercial educational purposes. Website: www.kendallhunt.com

Student Copy is on page 67.

A 3717 (Grade 7) Activating Background: Lee el título
a ti mismo. Luego dime qué crees que va a pasar en el
cuento.

Background: Low ├────────┼────────┤ High

La Inminente Amenaza

		MISCUES						
	Substitution	Insertion	Omission	Reversal	Repetition	Self-Correction of Unacceptable Miscue	Meaning Change (Significant Miscue)	
Bajo el caliente sol del clima tropical las — 8								
frentes de todo un grupo de hombres brillaban — 16								
del sudor causado por el esfuerzo que hacían por — 25								
caminar. Ellos eran guerrilleros que confiaban — 31								
totalmente en el líder que creían sería la — 39								
salvación de la patria. — 43								
Se habían propuesto llegar a una fortaleza — 50								
bastante distante y planeaban atacar el almacén — 57								
de la fortaleza con cohetes. Querían explotar la — 65								
dinamita como si fuera una pequeña caja de — 73								
fósforos encendidos. — 75								
Un hombre de tamaño impresionante dio una — 82								
órden mientras que ellos mantenían la ardua — 89								
marcha por la tierra deshabitada. Los — 95								
guerrilleros pretendían que el ataque causara tal — 102								
miedo en los soldados del fuerte que toda la — 111								
población del pueblo de seguro quedaría — 117								
convencida de la necesidad de unirse a la causa — 126								
de la guerrilla. — 129								
TOTAL								

Word Recognition Scoring Guide		
Total Miscues	Level	Significant Miscues
0–2	Independent	0–1
3–5	Ind./Inst.	2
6	Instructional	3
7–12	Inst./Frust.	4–5
13 +	Frustration	6 +

Total Miscues ☐   **Significant Miscues** ☐

Oral Reading Rate	Norm Group Percentile				
─── WPM)7740	☐ 90	☐ 75	☐ 50	☐ 25	☐ 10

A **3717** (Grade 7)
Comprehension Questions

T 1. _____ ¿De qué se trata esta historia?
(de un ataque a una fortaleza; de un
ataque a un fuerte; de un gran líder)

F 2. _____ ¿Qué clima hacía donde estaban los
guerrilleros?
(calor; mucho sol; un clima tropical)

F 3. _____ ¿Qué opinaban los guerrilleros de su
líder?
(creían que iba a salvar la patria;
confiaban totalmente en él)

F 4. _____ ¿Cómo era el terreno por donde los
guerrilleros caminaban?
(estaba deshabitado; era difícil de
atravesar)

F 5. _____ ¿Cuál era la meta de los guerrilleros?
(llegar a la fortaleza; atacar el
almacén; explotar la dinamita;
causarle miedo a los soldados)

F 6. _____ ¿Cómo planeaban destruir el almacén?
(explotando la dinamita)

F 7. _____ ¿Qué querían lograr en el ataque?
(causarle miedo a los soldados;
obtener el apoyo del pueblo;
convencer a la gente del pueblo que la
causa de ellos valía la pena; cualquier
respuesta lógica)

I 8. _____ ¿En qué país crees tú que esta historia
tuvo lugar?
(cualquier respuesta lógica que
sugiere un clima cálido)

E 9. _____ ¿A qué peligro se habrán enfrentado
los guerrilleros?
(cualquier respuesta lógica)

V 10. _____ ¿Qué significa la palabra *ardua*?
(duro; difícil; cualquier respuesta
lógica)

Retelling/Notes

☐ Questions Missed

Comprehension Scoring Guide	
Questions Missed	Level
0–1	Independent
1½–2	Ind./Inst.
2½	Instructional
3–4½	Inst./Frust.
5 +	Frustration

Retelling
Excellent
Satisfactory
Unsatisfactory

Student Copy is on page 68.

A 8183 (Grade 8) Activating Background: Lee el título a ti mismo. Luego dime qué crees que va a pasar en el cuento.

Background: Low |———+———| High

La Búsqueda del Científico

	Substitution	Insertion	Omission	Reversal	Repetition	Self-Correction of Unacceptable Miscue	Meaning Change (Significant Miscue)
MISCUES							
Cristóbal, un científico, trabajaba muy 5							
concentrado en el laboratorio. Alguien le había 12							
mandado una carta con una sugerencia muy 19							
interesante. La clave del éxito de su 26							
descubrimiento estaba en la precisión de la 33							
reacción del elemento químico que activaría la 40							
medicina que él se esforzaba por formular. 47							
Desde ese momento era cuestión de ir 54							
reduciéndo los diferentes componentes de la 60							
formula hasta identificar la cantidad necesaria 66							
para encontrar la fórmula ideal. 71							
Al fin y al cabo él estaba seguro de que lo 82							
lograría. Entonces tendría en sus manos el 89							
monopolio de la medicina que haría posible la 97							
immortalidad del ser humano. ¡Cristóbal sería la 104							
única persona que sabría la proporción de los 112							
productos químicos en cada pastilla! El eliminar 119							
la muerte y todas las enfermedades conocidas 126							
convertiría a Cristóbal en la persona más 133							
poderosa en la tierra. 137							
TOTAL							

Word Recognition Scoring Guide		
Total Miscues	Level	Significant Miscues
0–2	Independent	0–1
3–6	Ind./Inst.	2–3
7	Instructional	4
8–13	Inst./Frust.	5–6
14 +	Frustration	7 +

Total Miscues [ ]   **Significant Miscues** [ ]

Oral Reading Rate	Norm Group Percentile
——— WPM)8220	☐ 90 ☐ 75 ☐ 50 ☐ 25 ☐ 10

From Jerry L. Johns and Mayra C. Daniel, *Spanish Reading Inventory: Pre-Primer through Grade Eight* (2nd ed.). Copyright © 2010 by Kendall Hunt Publishing Company (1-800-247-3458). May be reproduced for noncommercial educational purposes. Website: www.kendallhunt.com

A **8183** (Grade 8)
Comprehension Questions

T 1. _____ ¿De qué se trata esta historia?
             (del esfuerzo de un científico)

F 2. _____ ¿ De dónde sacó el científico la
             idea de la fórmula?
             (de una carta)

F 3. _____ ¿Cuál era la clave del
             descubrimiento?
             (la reacción del elemento
             químico)

F 4. _____ ¿Qué ocurriría en la reacción?
             (se activaría la medicina; se vería
             el efecto de la fórmula)

F 5. _____ ¿Qué efectos tendría la medicina?
             (causaría la immortalidad)

F 6. _____ ¿Por qué creía Cristóbal que
             llegaría a ser poderoso?
             (sabría la fórmula)

F 7. _____ ¿Qué eliminaría la medicina?
             (la muerte; las enfermedades)

I 8. _____ ¿Cómo crees que la gente
             reaccionaría ante este
             descubrimiento?
             (cualquier respuesta lógica)

E 9. _____ ¿Crees que la vida de Cristóbal
             estaría en peligro luego de haber
             precisado la fórmula?
             (cualquier respuesta lógica)

V 10. _____ ¿Qué significa ser *immortal*?
             (vivir por siempre; no morir
             nunca; cualquier respuesta lógica)

Retelling/Notes

▢ Questions Missed

Comprehension Scoring Guide	
Questions Missed	Level
0–1	Independent
1$^{1}/_{2}$–2	Ind./Inst.
2$^{1}/_{2}$	Instructional
3–4$^{1}/_{2}$	Inst./Frust.
5 +	Frustration

Retelling
Excellent
Satisfactory
Unsatisfactory

Graded Word Lists
Student Copy

FORM **B**

Informational

List BB

1. mamá
2. sube
3. tela
4. piso
5. dos
6. mesa
7. foto
8. amo
9. casa
10. lobo
11. al
12. día
13. semana
14. famoso
15. bola
16. niño
17. ojo
18. venado
19. remo
20. leche

List B

1. hijo
2. silla
3. taza
4. cine
5. está
6. regalo
7. mañana
8. cuchillo
9. viejo
10. grande
11. hacen
12. zorro
13. chaqueta
14. buque
15. quería
16. agua
17. hija
18. gente
19. señor
20. juguete

List B 7141

1. globo
2. profesor
3. buscar
4. fresa
5. nuevo
6. terrible
7. libro
8. pequeño
9. trucha
10. primavera
11. hierro
12. blanco
13. claro
14. otro
15. causa
16. música
17. alegre
18. flores
19. peine
20. madrugada

List B 8224

1. frecuente
2. maravilla
3. venció
4. quisiera
5. negocio
6. esqueleto
7. abuelita
8. enciclopedia
9. miedoso
10. bolsillo
11. huellas
12. cuidado
13. eléctrica
14. por qué
15. todavía
16. necesitamos
17. buenísimo
18. albóndiga
19. enséñamelo
20. cómpramelo

List B 3183

1. cocuyo

2. barquito

3. conseguir

4. ebullición

5. paralelogramo

6. hormiguero

7. relámpago

8. zarigüeya

9. magnánimo

10. desahogarse

11. francotirador

12. costarricense

13. nicaragüense

14. solsticio

15. deslumbramiento

16. bodeguero

17. farmacéutico

18. oceanógrafo

19. monocotiledónio

20. polinización

Graded Passages
Student Copy

Informational

El Perro de Beto

Beto tiene un perro.
Se llama Lobo.
Lobo es un perro grande.

Lobo salta.
Beto le pasa la mano a Lobo.
Lobo es un perro muy divertido.

La Pelota Roja de Pedrín

"No puedo encontrar mi pelota,"
dijo Pedrín.
"Mi pelota es grande y roja."
"Veo una pelota," dijo Rosa.
"La pelota es azul. Es chiquita.
No es roja."

El Huevo de Ani

Hay una casa blanca en el bosque. Ani vive allí. A Ani le gusta el sol y el aire fresco. Ella decide dar un paseo. Ani encuentra algo por el camino en la hierba. Es redondo y blanco.

"Caramba" dice Ani. "¡Qué huevito tan lindo! Me lo llevo a la casa."

Su mamá está en la casa. Le dice a Ani.

"No puedes dejar que el huevo se enfríe."

Ani toma una caja y la llena de trapos viejos. Pone el huevo dentro. Pone la caja cerca de la estufa.

Al día siguiente Ani escucha un sonido que no conoce. "¡Pío, pío, pío!" El pollito ha nacido. Ahora Ani tiene una nueva mascota.

En el Zoológico

Daniel quería ir al zoológico. Le pidió permiso a su mamá. Ella le dijo que sí. Los dos fueron al zoológico. A Daniel le gustó mucho ver los animales. Un animal parecía tener dos colas. ¡Era un elefante! Otro animal tenía un lomo perfecto para dar un paseo. ¡Era una tortuga enorme! Daniel vio muchas cosas nuevas. Vio muchos animales peludos. Le causaron risa.

De pronto Daniel notó que casi era de noche. Daniel se puso a buscar a su mamá.

¡Estaba perdido! Se sentó y empezó a llorar. Pero cuando levantó la vista se sintió mejor. Su mamá venía corriendo hacia él.

Una Araña Amigable

Una araña se sentó al lado de un niño. El niño sintió miedo. No debió asustarse. La araña no le iba a hacer daño. Casi todas las arañas son buenas. Las arañas pertenecen a una familia de animales de ocho patas. Las arañas no son insectos.

En el otoño la mamá araña pone muchísimos huevos. Sólo sobreviven las arañitas fuertes. Cuando la primavera llega las arañitas dejan su nido. Comen hormigas y moscas. También comen muchos de los insectos que dañan las cosechas. Algunas arañas grandes comen ratas y pájaros. En muchas casas es fácil encontrar las telarañas que las arañas hacen con tanto trabajo.

El Canto del Grillo

Es una noche de verano. Trato de dormirme pero un sonido me despierta cada vez que me duermo. Es un grillo. Cuando los grillos cantan no usan la boca. El grillo varón tiene unas alas ásperas. Le gusta frotar un ala contra la otra. Las alas hacen sonidos.

Trato de encontrar el insecto pero me es difícil. El sonido no viene de un lugar. También no es fácil ver a los grillos. Estos pueden tener el tamaño de la uña del dedo pulgar. Algunos opinan que los grillos traen buena suerte. Tal vez a estas personas les gusta dormirse escuchando la canción del grillo.

Las Plantas Maravillosas

El mundo de las plantas es fascinante. Hay unas trescientas mil variedades de plantas. El oxígeno que respiramos viene de las plantas. Algunas crecen a ser más grandes que los animales y hasta viven más años que ellos.

Algunas plantas son más pequeñas que el punto final de esta oración. Estas se pueden ver únicamente con la ayuda de un microscopio. Otras, como el pino grande, son altas como rascacielos.

Casi todas las plantas tienen tallos y hojas. Las plantas viven en lugares diversos. Algunas hasta parecen crecer dentro de rocas. Otras viven en agua, sobre pan viejo, y hasta adentro de zapatos viejos.

El Vuelo

Los aviones de antes volaban con propelas.
Ahora, casi todos los aviones son jets. Algunos
vuelan más rápido que la velocidad del sonido.
Lo primero que uno ve al mirar un avión son
las alas grandes que los aviones tienen a
ambos lados.

Hoy día muchos aviones aterrizan y despegan
de grandes aeropuertos cada pocos segundos.
En un avión una persona puede atravesar largas
distancias en menos de una hora. A los viajeros
a veces les toma más tiempo recoger las maletas
al llegar a su destino que el tiempo que les toma
el vuelo.

Definitivamente, los aviones han mejorado
mucho desde que los hermanos Wright
volaron por primera vez en 1903.

Los Girasoles

Una de las flores más asombrosas que se
encuentra en la parte central de los Estados
Unidos es el girasol. Hay una leyenda que dice
que al girasol se le dio su nombre por su curiosa
costumbre de voltear la cabeza para darle frente
al sol.

El girasol es una planta muy fuerte. Su altura
puede medir tanto como una persona o más. La
cabeza del girasol se parece a la de la margarita.
Las dos tienen una circumferencia de pétalos
grandes y un círculo interno de pequeñas flores
de color café. Cuando estas pequeñas flores del
centro se secan, se convierten en las semillas del
girasol. Estas semillas producen unos patrones
que son únicos en su género en el mundo de las
plantas.

Celebraciones Indígenas

Los indígenas veneraban la majestuosidad de
la naturaleza como las estrellas, la luna y el sol.
En diferentes épocas del año honraban a un
poder supremo al que llamaban el Gran Espíritu.

Los días de fiesta celebraban ceremonias con
bailes y cenas suntuosas. Para estas ceremonias,
que duraban varios días, los indígenas se
decoraban el cuerpo y la cara y se vestían en sus
mejores atuendos. Cuando se reunían alrededor
del fuego del concilio, el curandero de cada tribu
guiaba la celebración. Los indígenas le rezaban
al Gran Espíritu y le pedían que les revelara sus
deseos enviándoles una señal.

Nuestro Medio Ambiente

Además de usar plantas y animales como alimentos, la piel de los animales se aprovecha para hacer zapatos, la madera de los árboles se usa para construir casas, las fibras de las plantas de algodón para hacer faldas y camisas, y la lana de las ovejas para telar hilo y tela para coser trajes y abrigos. Hasta las fibras sintéticas que son tan usadas en la industria provienen de materias naturales que hay en abundancia en nuestro medio ambiente.

El que digamos que el ser humano y el medio ambiente son interdependientes es una pequeña parte de este tema. En este milenio podemos llegar más lejos de lo que antes era posible y cambiar el medio ambiente usando conocimientos científicos y la tecnología. El ágil cerebro del ser humano nos facilita el que indaguemos profundamente en lo que la naturaleza pone a nuestro alcance.

Performance Booklet
Teacher Copy

Second Edition

SPANISH READING INVENTORY PERFORMANCE BOOKLET

Jerry L. Johns, Ph.D. & Mayra C. Daniel, Ed.D.

Form B

Student _____ Grade _____ Sex M F   Date of Test _____

School _____ Examiner _____ Date of Birth _____

Address _____ Current Book/Level_____ Age_____

SUMMARY OF STUDENT'S READING PERFORMANCE

Grade	Word Recognition							Comprehension		Reading Rate	
	Isolation (Word Lists)				Context (Passages)			Form B		Words per Minute (WPM)	Norm Group Per-centile
	Sight	Anal-ysis	Total	Level	Mis-cues	Level		Ques-tions Missed	Level		
PP1	■	■	■	■							
PP2											
P											
1											
2											
3											
4	■	■	■	■							
5	■	■	■	■							
6	■	■	■	■							
7	■	■	■	■							
8	■	■	■	■							

ESTIMATE OF READING LEVELS: Independent _____ Instructional _____ Frustration _____

LISTENING LEVEL

Grade	Form _____	
	Questions Missed	Level
1		
2		
3		
4		
5		
6		
7		
8		

ESTIMATED LEVEL: ____

GENERAL OBSERVATIONS

INFORMAL ANALYSIS OF ORAL READING

Oral Reading Behaviors	Frequency of Occurrence			General Impact on Meaning		
	Seldom	Sometimes	Frequently	No Change	Little Change	Much Change
Substitutions						
Insertions						
Omissions						
Reversals						
Repetitions						

QUALITATIVE ANALYSIS OF SPANISH READING INVENTORY INSIGHTS

General Directions: Note the degree to which the student shows behavior or evidence in the following areas. Space is provided for additional items.

	Seldom Weak Poor			Always Strong Excellent

COMPREHENSION

Seeks to construct meaning

Makes predictions

Activates background knowledge

Possesses appropriate concepts and vocabulary

Monitors reading

Varies reading rate as needed

Understands topic and major ideas

Remembers facts or details

Makes and supports appropriate inferences

Evaluates ideas from passages

Understands vocabulary used

Provides appropriate definitions of words

Engages with passages

_____

_____

WORD IDENTIFICATION

Possesses numerous strategies

Uses strategies flexibly

Uses graphophonic information

Uses semantic information

Uses syntactic information

Knows basic sight words automatically

Possesses sight vocabulary

_____

ORAL AND SILENT READING

Reads fluently

Reads with expression

Attends to punctuation

Keeps place while reading

Reads at appropriate rate

Reads silently without vocalization

_____

ATTITUDE AND CONFIDENCE

Enjoys reading

Demonstrates willingness to risk

Possesses positive self-concept

Chooses to read

Regards himself/herself as a reader

Exhibits persistence

_____

Form B • Graded Word Lists • Performance Booklet • Student Copy is on page 98.

List BB (Pre-Primer)	Sight	Analysis	List B (Primer)	Sight	Analysis
1. mamá			1. hijo		
2. sube			2. silla		
3. tela			3. taza		
4. piso			4. cine		
5. dos			5. está		
6. mesa			6. regalo		
7. foto			7. mañana		
8. amo			8. cuchillo		
9. casa			9. viejo		
10. lobo			10. grande		
11. al			11. hacen		
12. día			12. zorro		
13. semana			13. chaqueta		
14. famoso			14. buque		
15. bola			15. quería		
16. niño			16. agua		
17. ojo			17. hija		
18. venado			18. gente		
19. remo			19. señor		
20. leche			20. juguete		
Number Correct			Number Correct		
Total			Total		

Scoring Guide for Graded Word Lists			
Independent	Instructional	Inst./Frust.	Frustration
20 19	18 17 16	15 14	13 or less

From Jerry L. Johns and Mayra C. Daniel, *Spanish Reading Inventory: Pre-Primer through Grade Eight* (2nd ed.). Copyright © 2010 by Kendall Hunt Publishing Company (1-800-247-3458). May be reproduced for noncommercial educational purposes. Website: www.kendallhunt.com

Form B • Graded Word Lists • Performance Booklet • Student Copy is on page 99.

List B 7141 (Grade 1)	Sight	Analysis	List B 8224 (Grade 2)	Sight	Analysis
1. globo	_____	_____	1. frecuente	_____	_____
2. profesor	_____	_____	2. maravilla	_____	_____
3. buscar	_____	_____	3. venció	_____	_____
4. fresa	_____	_____	4. quisiera	_____	_____
5. nuevo	_____	_____	5. negocio	_____	_____
6. terrible	_____	_____	6. esqueleto	_____	_____
7. libro	_____	_____	7. abuelita	_____	_____
8. pequeño	_____	_____	8. enciclopedia	_____	_____
9. trucha	_____	_____	9. miedoso	_____	_____
10. primavera	_____	_____	10. bolsillo	_____	_____
11. hierro	_____	_____	11. huellas	_____	_____
12. blanco	_____	_____	12. cuidado	_____	_____
13. claro	_____	_____	13. eléctrica	_____	_____
14. otro	_____	_____	14. por qué	_____	_____
15. causa	_____	_____	15. todavía	_____	_____
16. música	_____	_____	16. necesitamos	_____	_____
17. alegre	_____	_____	17. buenísimo	_____	_____
18. flores	_____	_____	18. albóndiga	_____	_____
19. peine	_____	_____	19. enséñamelo	_____	_____
20. madrugada	_____	_____	20. cómpramelo	_____	_____
Number Correct	_____	_____	Number Correct	_____	_____
Total	_____		Total	_____	

Scoring Guide for Graded Word Lists			
Independent	Instructional	Inst./Frust.	Frustration
20 19	18 17 16	15 14	13 or less

List B 3183
(Grade 3)

	Sight	**Analysis**
1. cocuyo	_____	_____
2. barquito	_____	_____
3. conseguir	_____	_____
4. ebullición	_____	_____
5. paralelogramo	_____	_____
6. hormiguero	_____	_____
7. relámpago	_____	_____
8. zarigüeya	_____	_____
9. magnánimo	_____	_____
10. desahogarse	_____	_____
11. francotirador	_____	_____
12. costarricense	_____	_____
13. nicaragüense	_____	_____
14. solsticio	_____	_____
15. deslumbramiento	_____	_____
16. bodeguero	_____	_____
17. farmacéutico	_____	_____
18. oceanógrafo	_____	_____
19. monocotiledónio	_____	_____
20. polinización	_____	_____

Number Correct _____ _____

Total _____

Scoring Guide for Graded Word Lists			
Independent	Instructional	Inst./Frust.	Frustration
20 19	18 17 16	15 14	13 or less

Student Copy is on page 102.

BBB (Pre-Primer 1) Activating Background: Lee el título a ti mismo. Luego dime qué crees que va a pasar en el cuento.

Background: Low ├─────┼─────┤ High

El Perro de Beto		MISCUES					Self-Correction of Unacceptable Miscue	Meaning Change (Significant Miscue)
		Substitution	Insertion	Omission	Reversal	Repetition		
Beto tiene un perro.	4							
Se llama Lobo.	7							
Lobo es un perro grande.	12							
Lobo salta.	14							
Beto le pasa la mano a Lobo.	21							
Lobo es un perro muy divertido.	27							
TOTAL								

Total Miscues [ ]   Significant Miscues [ ]

Word Recognition Scoring Guide		
Total Miscues	Level	Significant Miscues
0	Independent	0
1	Ind./Inst.	—
2	Instructional	1
3	Inst./Frust.	2
4 +	Frustration	3 +

Oral Reading Rate	Norm Group Percentile
⎯⎯⎯ WPM)1620	☐ 90 ☐ 75 ☐ 50 ☐ 25 ☐ 10

From Jerry L. Johns and Mayra C. Daniel, *Spanish Reading Inventory: Pre-Primer through Grade Eight* (2nd ed.). Copyright © 2010 by Kendall Hunt Publishing Company (1-800-247-3458). May be reproduced for noncommercial educational purposes. Website: www.kendallhunt.com

BBB (Pre-Primer 1)
Comprehension Questions

F 1. _____ ¿Cómo se llama el perro?
            (Lobo)

F 2. _____ ¿De qué tamaño es Lobo?
            (grande)

E 3. _____ ¿Por qué es Lobo un perro
            divertido?
            (cualquier respuesta lógica, salta,
            etc.)

I 4. _____ ¿Qué más le gustará hacer a
            Lobo?
            (cualquier respuesta lógica;
            correr, dormir con Beto)

V 5. _____ ¿Qué quiere decir *ser divertido*?
            (cualquier repuesta lógica; ser
            cómico; ser agradable)

Retelling/Notes

☐ Questions Missed

Comprehension Scoring Guide	
Questions Missed	Level
0	Independent
1	Ind./Inst.
1½	Instructional
2	Inst./Frust.
2½ +	Frustration

Retelling
Excellent
Satisfactory
Unsatisfactory

From Jerry L. Johns and Mayra C. Daniel, *Spanish Reading Inventory: Pre-Primer through Grade Eight* (2nd ed.). Copyright © 2010 by Kendall Hunt Publishing Company (1-800-247-3458). May be reproduced for noncommercial educational purposes. Website: www.kendallhunt.com

Student Copy is on page 103.

BB (Pre-Primer 2) Activating Background: Lee el título a ti mismo. Luego dime qué crees que va a pasar en el cuento.

Background: Low ├────┼────┤ High

La Pelota Roja de Pedrín		Substitution	Insertion	Omission	Reversal	Repetition	Self-Correction of Unacceptable Miscue	Meaning Change (Significant Miscue)
		MISCUES						
"No puedo encontrar mi pelota,"	5							
dijo Pedrín.	7							
"Mi pelota es grande y roja."	13							
"Veo una pelota," dijo Rosa.	18							
"La pelota es azul. Es chiquita.	24							
No es roja."	27							
TOTAL								

Total Miscues ☐   Significant Miscues ☐

Word Recognition Scoring Guide		
Total Miscues	Level	Significant Miscues
0	Independent	0
1	Ind./Inst.	—
2	Instructional	1
3	Inst./Frust.	2
4 +	Frustration	3 +

Oral Reading Rate	Norm Group Percentile
⎯⎯⎯ WPM)1620	☐ 90 ☐ 75 ☐ 50 ☐ 25 ☐ 10

BB (Pre-Primer 2)
Comprehension Questions

F 1. _____ ¿Qué le pasó a Pedrín?
(se le perdió la pelota)

F 2. _____ ¿Cómo era la pelota que encontró
Rosa?
(azul y pequeña)

E 3. _____ ¿Qué juego jugará Pedrín con su
pelota?
(cualquier respuesta lógica)

I 4. _____ ¿Por qué sabía Pedrín que la
pelota que Rosa tenía no era
suya?
(no era roja; era pequeña y azul;
cualquier respuesta lógica)

V 5. _____ ¿Qué es *una pelota*?
(algo con que juegas; es redonda;
cualquier respuesta lógica)

Retelling/Notes

Questions Missed

Comprehension Scoring Guide	
Questions Missed	Level
0	Independent
1	Ind./Inst.
1¹/₂	Instructional
2	Inst./Frust.
2¹/₂ +	Frustration

Retelling
Excellent
Satisfactory
Unsatisfactory

Student Copy is on page 104.

B (Primer) Activating Background: Lee el título a ti mismo. Luego dime qué crees que va a pasar en el cuento.

Background: Low ├──────┼──────┤ High

El Huevo de Ani		Substitution	Insertion	Omission	Reversal	Repetition	Self-Correction of Unacceptable Miscue	Meaning Change (Significant Miscue)
Hay una casa blanca en el bosque. Ani vive	9							
allí. A Ani le gusta el sol y el aire fresco. Ella	21							
decide dar un paseo. Ani encuentra algo por el	30							
camino en la hierba. Es redondo y blanco.	38							
"Caramba" dice Ani. "¡Qué huevito tan	44							
lindo! Me lo llevo a la casa."	51							
Su mamá está en la casa. Le dice a Ani.	61							
"No puedes dejar que el huevo se enfríe."	69							
Ani toma una caja y la llena de trapos	78							
viejos. Pone el huevo dentro. Pone la caja	86							
cerca de la estufa.	90							
Al día siguiente Ani escucha un sonido que	98							
no conoce. "¡Pío, pío, pío!" El pollito ha	106							
nacido. Ahora Ani tiene una nueva	112							
mascota.	113							
TOTAL								

MISCUES

Total Miscues ☐   Significant Miscues ☐

Word Recognition Scoring Guide		
Total Miscues	Level	Significant Miscues
0	Independent	0
1–2	Ind./Inst.	1
3	Instructional	2
4	Inst./Frust.	3
5 +	Frustration	4 +

Oral Reading Rate	Norm Group Percentile
WPM)6780	☐ 90 ☐ 75 ☐ 50 ☐ 25 ☐ 10

B (Primer)
Comprehension Questions

T 1. _____ ¿De qué se tratá este cuento?
(de Ani, una niña que encuentra un huevo)

F 2. _____ ¿Dónde vive Ani?
(en el bosque; en una casa blanca)

F 3. _____ ¿Qué le da gusto a Ani?
(el sol; el aire fresco; encontrar un huevo)

F 4. _____ ¿Qué hace Ani?
(da un paseo; encuentra un huevo)

F 5. _____ ¿Dónde encuentra Ani el huevo?
(en el camino; en la hierba)

F 6. _____ ¿Qué hace Ani para que no se enfríe el huevo?
(lo pone en una caja llena de trapos viejos; pone el huevo cerca de una estufa)

I 7. _____ ¿Cómo crees que el huevo llegó a estar en la hierba?
(cualquier respuesta lógica)

I 8. _____ ¿Por qué era importante que el huevo estuviera caliente?
(cualquier respuesta lógica; para que naciera el pollito)

E 9. _____ ¿Qué otras cosas podría haber encontrado Ani en su paseo?
(cualquier respuesta lógica; animales, hojas, piedras, plantas, otros huevos, etc.)

V 10. _____ ¿Qué es *una estufa*?
(algo que calienta la comida; algo que se usa para cocinar; cualquier respuesta lógica)

Retelling/Notes

[ ] Questions Missed

Comprehension Scoring Guide	
Questions Missed	Level
0–1	Independent
1½–2	Ind./Inst.
2½	Instructional
3–4½	Inst./Frust.
5 +	Frustration

Retelling
Excellent
Satisfactory
Unsatisfactory

From Jerry L. Johns and Mayra C. Daniel, *Spanish Reading Inventory: Pre-Primer through Grade Eight* (2nd ed.). Copyright © 2010 by Kendall Hunt Publishing Company (1-800-247-3458). May be reproduced for noncommercial educational purposes. Website: www.kendallhunt.com

Student Copy is on page 105.

B 7141 (Grade 1) Activating Background: Lee el título a ti mismo. Luego dime qué crees que va a pasar en el cuento.

Background: Low |———+———| High

En el Zoológico		Substitution	Insertion	Omission	Reversal	Repetition	Self-Correction of Unacceptable Miscue	Meaning Change (Significant Miscue)
MISCUES								
Daniel quería ir al zoológico. Le pidió	7							
permiso a su mamá. Ella le dijo que sí.	16							
Los dos fueron al zoológico. A Daniel le	24							
gustó mucho ver los animales. Un animal	31							
parecía tener dos colas. ¡Era un elefante!	38							
Otro animal tenía un lomo perfecto para dar	46							
un paseo. ¡Era una tortuga enorme! Daniel vio	54							
muchas cosas nuevas. Vio muchos animales	60							
peludos. Le causaron risa.	64							
De pronto Daniel notó que casi era de	72							
noche. Daniel se puso a buscar a su mamá.	81							
¡Estaba perdido! Se sentó y empezó a	88							
llorar. Pero cuando levantó la vista se	95							
sintió mejor. Su mamá venía corriendo	101							
hacia él.	103							
TOTAL								

Total Miscues [ ]   Significant Miscues [ ]

Word Recognition Scoring Guide		
Total Miscues	Level	Significant Miscues
0–1	Independent	0–1
2–4	Ind./Inst.	2
5	Instructional	3
6–9	Inst./Frust.	4
10 +	Frustration	5 +

Oral Reading Rate	Norm Group Percentile
⟌6180 WPM	☐ 90 ☐ 75 ☐ 50 ☐ 25 ☐ 10

B 7141 (Grade 1)
Comprehension Questions

T   1. _____ ¿De qué se trata este cuento?
(de un niño que va a un zoológico)

F   2. _____ ¿Quién fue con Daniel?
(su mamá; su madre)

F   3. _____ Daniel pensó que el lomo de la
tortuga estaba perfecto para hacer
algo. ¿Para qué pensó que el lomo
estaba perfecto?
(para dar un paseo; para montarse)

F   4. _____ ¿Qué otros animales vio Daniel en
el zoológico?
(un elefante; animales peludos)

F   5. _____ ¿Qué pensó Daniel del elefante
cuando lo vio por primera vez?
(que tenía dos colas; cualquier
respuesta lógica)

F   6. _____ ¿Qué vio Daniel cuando levantó la
vista y ya era casi de noche?
(vio a su mamá; vio que su mamá
venia corriendo hacia él)

I   7. _____ ¿Por qué piensas que Daniel quería
ir al zoológico?
(cualquier respuesta lógica)

I   8. _____ ¿Cuáles eran los animales peludos?
(cualquier respuesta lógica; los
monos; los osos, etc.)

I   9. _____ ¿Qué crees que los animales
peludos habrán hecho para causarle
risa a Daniel?
(cualquier respuesta lógica)

V   10. _____ ¿Qué quiere decir la palabra
peludo?
(tener mucho pelo; demasiado pelo)

Retelling/Notes

☐ Questions Missed

Comprehension Scoring Guide	
Questions Missed	Level
0–1	Independent
1½–2	Ind./Inst.
2½	Instructional
3–4½	Inst./Frust.
5 +	Frustration

Retelling
Excellent
Satisfactory
Unsatisfactory

Student Copy is on page 106.

B 8224 (Grade 2) Activating Background: Lee el título a ti mismo. Luego dime qué crees que va a pasar en el cuento.

Background: Low ├────┼────┤ High

Una Araña Amigable		MISCUES							
		Substitution	Insertion	Omission	Reversal	Repetition	Self-Correction of Unacceptable Miscue	Meaning Change (Significant Miscue)	
Una araña se sentó al lado de un niño. El	10								
niño sintió miedo. No debió asustarse. La	17								
araña no le iba a hacer daño. Casi todas las	27								
arañas son buenas. Las arañas pertenecen a	34								
una familia de animales de ocho patas. Las	42								
arañas no son insectos.	46								
En el otoño la mamá araña pone muchísimos	54								
huevos. Sólo sobreviven las arañitas	59								
fuertes. Cuando la primavera llega las	65								
arañitas dejan su nido. Comen hormigas y	72								
moscas. También comen muchos de los	78								
insectos que dañan las cosechas. Algunas	84								
arañas grandes comen ratas y pájaros. En	91								
muchas casas es fácil encontrar las	97								
telarañas que las arañas hacen con tanto	104								
trabajo.	105								
TOTAL									

Word Recognition Scoring Guide		
Total Miscues	Level	Significant Miscues
0–2	Independent	0–1
3–5	Ind./Inst.	2
6	Instructional	3
7–11	Inst./Frust.	4–5
12 +	Frustration	6 +

Total Miscues [ ]   **Significant Miscues** [ ]

Oral Reading Rate	Norm Group Percentile
6360)‾‾ WPM	☐ 90 ☐ 75 ☐ 50 ☐ 25 ☐ 10

B 8224 (Grade 2)
Comprehension Questions

T 1. _____ ¿De qué se trata este cuento?
(de las arañas)

F 2. _____ ¿Qué fue lo primero que la araña
en este cuento hizo?
(se sentó al lado de un niño)

F 3. _____ ¿Cuántas patas tiene una araña?
(ocho)

F 4. _____ ¿Cuándo ponen sus huevos las
arañas madres?
(en el otoño)

F 5. _____ ¿Cuántos huevos puede poner una
mamá araña?
(muchísimos)

F 6. _____ ¿Qué comen las arañas?
(hormigas; moscas; insectos; ratas;
pájaros; cualquier dos respuestas)

E 7. _____ ¿Dónde crees que las arañas
encuentran su comida?
(cualquier respuesta lógica; en el
campo, en la telaraña)

I 8. _____ ¿Qué le pasará a las arañas que
nacen débiles?
(cualquier respuesta lógica; se
mueren; se enferman)

I 9. _____ ¿Por qué piensas que la gente le
tiene miedo a las arañas?
(cualquier respuesta lógica)

V 10. _____ ¿Cómo es *la telaraña* que la araña
hace?
(cualquier respuesta lógica; es
bonita; es como una tela)

Retelling/Notes

☐ Questions Missed

Comprehension Scoring Guide	
Questions Missed	Level
0–1	Independent
1½–2	Ind./Inst.
2½	Instructional
3–4½	Inst./Frust.
5 +	Frustration

Retelling
Excellent
Satisfactory
Unsatisfactory

From Jerry L. Johns and Mayra C. Daniel, *Spanish Reading Inventory: Pre-Primer through Grade Eight* (2nd ed.). Copyright © 2010 by Kendall Hunt Publishing Company (1-800-247-3458). May be reproduced for noncommercial educational purposes. Website: www.kendallhunt.com

Student Copy is on page 107.

B 3183 (Grade 3) Activating Background: Lee el título a ti mismo. Luego dime qué crees que va a pasar en el cuento.

Background: Low ├────────┼────────┤ High

El Canto del Grillo		Substitution	Insertion	Omission	Reversal	Repetition	Self-Correction of Unacceptable Miscue	Meaning Change (Significant Miscue)
		MISCUES						
Es una noche de verano. Trato de	7							
dormirme pero un sonido me despierta cada vez	15							
que me duermo. Es un grillo. Cuando los grillos	24							
cantan no usan la boca. El grillo varón tiene unas	34							
alas ásperas. Le gusta frotar un ala contra la	43							
otra. Las alas hacen sonidos.	48							
Trato de encontrar el insecto pero me es	56							
difícil. El sonido no viene de un lugar.	64							
También no es fácil ver a los grillos. Estos	73							
pueden tener el tamaño de la uña del dedo	82							
pulgar. Algunos opinan que los grillos	88							
traen buena suerte. Tal vez a estas	95							
personas les gusta dormirse escuchando la	101							
canción del grillo.	104							
TOTAL								

Total Miscues [ ]   Significant Miscues [ ]

Word Recognition Scoring Guide		
Total Miscues	Level	Significant Miscues
0–1	Independent	0–1
2–4	Ind./Inst.	2
5	Instructional	3
6–9	Inst./Frust.	5
10 +	Frustration	5 +

Oral Reading Rate	Norm Group Percentile
6240 ⟌ ___ WPM	☐ 90 ☐ 75 ☐ 50 ☐ 25 ☐ 10

B 3183 (Grade 3)
Comprehension Questions

| | | Retelling/Notes |

T   1. _____ ¿De qué se trata este cuento?
(de un grillo; de cómo un grillo canta;
de cómo los grillos se frotan las alas)

F   2. _____ ¿Cuándo ocurre este cuento?
(por la noche; en el verano)

F   3. _____ ¿Por qué no puede dormir la persona
que cuenta este cuento?
(por el sonido que hace el grillo; por
el canto del grillo; por el ruido)

F   4. _____ ¿Cómo produce el grillo su sonido?
(frota un ala contra la otra; frota las
alas unas con otras)

F   5. _____ ¿Qué clase de grillo hace el sonido?
(el macho; el varón; el papá)

F   6. _____ ¿Por qué es difícil encontrar el origen
del sonido del grillo?
(el sonido no viene de un solo lado; el
grillo es pequeño; es difícil ver dónde
está el grillo)

I   7. _____ ¿Por qué supones que sólo el macho
hace el sonido?
(cualquier respuesta lógica; así son;
las hembras no pueden hacer el
sonido)

I   8. _____ ¿Por qué piensas que alguna gente
cree que los grillos traen buena
suerte?
(cualquier respuesta lógica)

E   9. _____ ¿Cómo te sentirías tú si un grillo no te
dejara dormir? ¿Por qué?
(cualquier respuesta lógica; cansado;
enojado)

V   10. _____ ¿Qué es *el pulgar*?
(un dedo de la mano)

☐ Questions Missed

Comprehension Scoring Guide	
Questions Missed	Level
0–1	Independent
1½–2	Ind./Inst.
2½	Instructional
3–4½	Inst./Frust.
5 +	Frustration

Retelling
Excellent
Satisfactory
Unsatisfactory

Student Copy is on page 108.

B 5414 (Grade 4) Activating Background: Lee el título a ti mismo. Luego dime qué crees que va a pasar en el cuento.

Background: Low ⊢————┼————⊣ High

Las Plantas Maravillosas

		MISCUES						
	Substitution	Insertion	Omission	Reversal	Repetition	Self-Correction of Unacceptable Miscue	Meaning Change (Significant Miscue)
El mundo de las plantas es fascinante. Hay 8							
unas trescientas mil variedades de plantas. 14							
El oxígeno que respiramos viene de las 21							
plantas. Algunas crecen a ser más grandes 28							
que los animales y hasta viven más años 36							
que ellos. 38							
Algunas plantas son más pequeñas que el 45							
punto final de esta oración. Estas se pueden 53							
ver únicamente con la ayuda de un 60							
microscopio. Otras, como el pino grande, 66							
son altas como rascacielos. 70							
Casi todas las plantas tienen tallos y hojas. Las 79							
plantas viven en lugares diversos. Algunas hasta 86							
parecen crecer dentro de rocas. Otras viven en 94							
agua, sobre pan viejo, y hasta adentro de zapatos 103							
viejos. 104							
TOTAL							

Word Recognition Scoring Guide		
Total Miscues	Level	Significant Miscues
0–1	Independent	0–1
2–4	Ind./Inst.	2
5	Instructional	3
6–9	Inst./Frust.	4
10 +	Frustration	5 +

Total Miscues [ ]   Significant Miscues [ ]

Oral Reading Rate	Norm Group Percentile
6240)‾‾ WPM	☐ 90 ☐ 75 ☐ 50 ☐ 25 ☐ 10

From Jerry L. Johns and Mayra C. Daniel, *Spanish Reading Inventory: Pre-Primer through Grade Eight* (2nd ed.). Copyright © 2010 by Kendall Hunt Publishing Company (1-800-247-3458). May be reproduced for noncommercial educational purposes. Website: www.kendallhunt.com

B 5414 (Grade 4)
Comprehension Questions

<table>
<tr><td></td><td></td><td></td><td></td><td rowspan="20" style="border: 1px solid black;">**Retelling/Notes**</td></tr>
</table>

T   1. _____ ¿De qué se trata esta lectura?
(del mundo de las plantas)

F   2. _____ ¿Cuántas especies de plantas hay?
(mas de 300.000)

F   3. _____ ¿Qué tan pequeña puede ser una planta?
(más pequeña que un punto; tan pequeñas que hay que usar un microscopio para verlas)

F   4. _____ ¿Cómo son la mayor parte de las plantas?
(tienen tallo y hojas; cualquier respuesta lógica)

F   5. _____ Según la lectura, ¿dónde pueden vivir las plantas?
(en agua; en pan; en zapatos; en lugares diversos; cualquier dos repuestas)

F   6. _____ ¿Qué se usa para ver las plantas pequeñas?
(un microscopio)

I   7. _____ Dime el nombre de algunas plantas que viven por más tiempo que la mayoria de los animales.
(los árboles; los pinos; cualquier respuesta lógica)

I   8. _____ ¿Por qué se interesaría una persona en estudiar el mundo de las plantas?
(cualquier respuesta lógica; sería divertido; hay muchas plantas)

E   9. _____ ¿Qué crees que pasaría si se murieran todas las plantas? ¿Por qué crees esto?
(cualquier respuesta lógica; nadie viviría; no habría nada en el mundo)

V 10. _____ ¿Qué es *un microscopio*?
(cualquier respuesta lógica; un aparato que se usa para ver cosas muy pequeñas; algo que hay en la escuela)

Retelling/Notes

☐ Questions Missed

Comprehension Scoring Guide	
Questions Missed	Level
0–1	Independent
1½–2	Ind./Inst.
2½	Instructional
3–4½	Inst./Frust.
5 +	Frustration

Retelling
Excellent
Satisfactory
Unsatisfactory

Student Copy is on page 109.

B 8595 (Grade 5) Activating Background: Lee el título a ti mismo. Luego dime qué crees que va a pasar en el cuento.

Background: Low ├──────┼──────┤ High

El Vuelo

		MISCUES						
	Substitution	Insertion	Omission	Reversal	Repetition	Self-Correction of Unacceptable Miscue	Meaning Change (Significant Miscue)	
Los aviones de antes volaban con propelas. 7								
Ahora, casi todos los aviones son jets. Algunos 15								
vuelan más rápido que la velocidad del sonido. 23								
Lo primero que uno ve al mirar un avión son 33								
las alas grandes que los aviones tienen a 41								
ambos lados. 43								
Hoy día muchos aviones aterrizan y despegan 50								
de grandes aeropuertos cada pocos segundos. 56								
En un avión una persona puede atravesar largas 64								
distancias en menos de una hora. A los viajeros 73								
a veces les toma más tiempo recoger las maletas 82								
al llegar a su destino que el tiempo que les toma 93								
el vuelo. 95								
Definitivamente, los aviones han mejorado 100								
mucho desde que los hermanos Wright 106								
volaron por primera vez en 1903. 112								
TOTAL								

Word Recognition Scoring Guide		
Total Miscues	Level	Significant Miscues
0–1	Independent	0–1
2–4	Ind./Inst.	2
5	Instructional	3
6–11	Inst./Frust.	4–5
12 +	Frustration	6 +

Total Miscues ☐   Significant Miscues ☐

Oral Reading Rate	Norm Group Percentile
‾‾‾‾ WPM 6720⟌	☐ 90 ☐ 75 ☐ 50 ☐ 25 ☐ 10

B 8595 (Grade 5)
Comprehension Questions

<table>
<tr><td>T</td><td>1. _____</td><td>¿De qué se trata este cuento?
(de los aviones; de los cambios en los aviones; de cómo los aviones vuelan de rapido)</td></tr>
<tr><td>F</td><td>2. _____</td><td>¿Qué clase de motor tienen los aviones ahora?
(motores de propulsión a chorro; tienen jets; cualquier respuesta lógica)</td></tr>
<tr><td>F</td><td>3. _____</td><td>¿Cuán rápido pueden volar algunos aviones?
(cualquier respuesta lógica; más rápido que la velocidad del sonido)</td></tr>
<tr><td>F</td><td>4. _____</td><td>¿Cómo volaban los aviones de antes?
(con propelas; con alas que se movian; cualquier respuesta lógica)</td></tr>
<tr><td>F</td><td>5. _____</td><td>¿Qué año volaron los hermanos Wright por primera vez?
(1903)</td></tr>
<tr><td>F</td><td>6. _____</td><td>Según este cuento, ¿en cuánto tiempo puede una persona volar largas distancias?
(menos de uns hora; cualquier respuesta lógica)</td></tr>
<tr><td>F</td><td>7. _____</td><td>Según este cuento, ¿con cuánta frecuencia despegan y aterrizan aviones en los grandes aeropuertos?
(cada pocos segundos; cualquier respuesta lógica)</td></tr>
<tr><td>I</td><td>8. _____</td><td>¿Cómo crees que los hermanos Wright se habrán sentido después de su primer vuelo?
(cualquier respuesta lógica)</td></tr>
<tr><td>E</td><td>9. _____</td><td>¿Crees que los aviones han mejorado nuestras vidas? ¿Por qué?
(cualquier respuesta lógica)</td></tr>
<tr><td>V</td><td>10. _____</td><td>¿Qué significa llegar a su destino?
(cualquier respuesta lógica)</td></tr>
</table>

Retelling/Notes

☐ Questions Missed

Comprehension Scoring Guide	
Questions Missed	Level
0–1	Independent
1½–2	Ind./Inst.
2½	Instructional
3–4½	Inst./Frust.
5 +	Frustration

Retelling
Excellent
Satisfactory
Unsatisfactory

Student Copy is on page 110.

B 6867 (Grade 6) Activating Background: Lee el título a ti mismo. Luego dime qué crees que va a pasar en el cuento.

Background: Low |———+———| High

Los Girasoles		Substitution	Insertion	Omission	Reversal	Repetition	Self-Correction of Unacceptable Miscue	Meaning Change (Significant Miscue)
		MISCUES						
Una de las flores más asombrosas que se	8							
encuentra en la parte central de los Estados	16							
Unidos es el girasol. Hay una leyenda que dice	25							
que al girasol se le dio su nombre por su curiosa	36							
costumbre de voltear la cabeza para darle frente	44							
al sol.	46							
El girasol es una planta muy fuerte. Su altura	55							
puede medir tanto como una persona o más. La	64							
cabeza del girasol se parece a la de la margarita.	74							
Las dos tienen una circumferencia de pétalos	81							
grandes y un círculo interno de pequeñas flores	89							
de color café. Cuando estas pequeñas flores del	97							
centro se secan, se convierten en las semillas del	106							
girasol. Estas semillas producen unos patrones	112							
que son únicos en su género en el mundo de las	123							
plantas.	124							
TOTAL								

Word Recognition Scoring Guide

Total Miscues	Level	Significant Miscues
0–2	Independent	0–1
3–5	Ind./Inst.	2
6	Instructional	3
7–12	Inst./Frust.	4–5
13 +	Frustration	6 +

Total Miscues [ ]   **Significant Miscues** [ ]

Oral Reading Rate	Norm Group Percentile
7380)‾‾‾‾‾ WPM	☐ 90 ☐ 75 ☐ 50 ☐ 25 ☐ 10

From Jerry L. Johns and Mayra C. Daniel, *Spanish Reading Inventory: Pre-Primer through Grade Eight* (2nd ed.). Copyright © 2010 by Kendall Hunt Publishing Company (1-800-247-3458). May be reproduced for noncommercial educational purposes. Website: www.kendallhunt.com

B 6867 (Grade 6)
Comprehension Questions

T   1. _____ ¿De qué se tratan estos párrafos?
(de los girasoles)

F   2. _____ ¿De dónde sacó el girasol su nombre?
(porque voltea la cabeza hacia el sol)

F   3. _____ ¿A qué altura crece el girasol?
(crece tanto como una persona o más)

F   4. _____ ¿Qué tiene el girasol por el borde?
(pétalos)

F   5. _____ ¿De qué colores es el círculo del centro del girasol?
(color café)

F   6. _____ ¿A qué flor se parece la cabeza del girasol?
(a la margarita)

F   7. _____ ¿Qué producen las pequeñas flores del centro del girasol?
(semillas)

I   8. _____ ¿Es posible que algunos girasoles sean más grandes que tú?
(cualquier respuesta lógica)

E   9. _____ ¿Por qué crees que un girasol podría considerarse una planta fuerte?
(cualquier respuesta lógica; tiene un tallo largo; tiene un tallo grueso)

V 10. _____ ¿Qué significa *unos patrones únicos*?
(un dibujo que se repite; el diseño de la flor; cualquier respuesta lógica)

Retelling/Notes

☐ Questions Missed

Comprehension Scoring Guide	
Questions Missed	Level
0–1	Independent
1½–2	Ind./Inst.
2½	Instructional
3–4½	Inst./Frust.
5 +	Frustration

Retelling
Excellent
Satisfactory
Unsatisfactory

From Jerry L. Johns and Mayra C. Daniel, *Spanish Reading Inventory: Pre-Primer through Grade Eight* (2nd ed.). Copyright © 2010 by Kendall Hunt Publishing Company (1-800-247-3458). May be reproduced for noncommercial educational purposes. Website: www.kendallhunt.com

Student Copy is on page 111.

B 3717 (Grade 7) Activating Background: Lee el título a ti mismo. Luego dime qué crees que va a pasar en el cuento.

Background: Low |————+————| High

Celebraciones Indígenas

		MISCUES						
	Substitution	Insertion	Omission	Reversal	Repetition	Self-Correction of Unacceptable Miscue	Meaning Change (Significant Miscue)	
Los indígenas veneraban la majestuosidad de	6							
la naturaleza como las estrellas, la luna y el sol.	16							
En diferentes épocas del año honraban a un	24							
poder supremo al que llamaban el Gran Espíritu.	32							
Los días de fiesta celebraban ceremonias con	39							
bailes y cenas suntuosas. Para estas ceremonias,	46							
que duraban varios días, los indígenas se	53							
decoraban el cuerpo y la cara y se vestían en sus	64							
mejores atuendos. Cuando se reunían alrededor	70							
del fuego del concilio, el curandero de cada tribu	79							
guiaba la celebración. Los indígenas le rezaban	86							
al Gran Espíritu y le pedían que les revelara sus	96							
deseos enviándoles una señal.	100							
TOTAL								

Total Miscues ☐   Significant Miscues ☐

Word Recognition Scoring Guide		
Total Miscues	Level	Significant Miscues
0–1	Independent	0–1
2–4	Ind./Inst.	2
5	Instructional	3
6–9	Inst./Frust.	4
10 +	Frustration	5 +

Oral Reading Rate	Norm Group Percentile
——— WPM)6000	☐ 90 ☐ 75 ☐ 50 ☐ 25 ☐ 10

From Jerry L. Johns and Mayra C. Daniel, *Spanish Reading Inventory: Pre-Primer through Grade Eight* (2nd ed.). Copyright © 2010 by Kendall Hunt Publishing Company (1-800-247-3458). May be reproduced for noncommercial educational purposes. Website: www.kendallhunt.com

B 3717 (Grade 7)
Comprehension Questions

<table>
<tr><td></td><td></td><td></td><td style="text-align:center">Retelling/Notes</td></tr>
</table>

T   1. _____ ¿De qué se trata este cuento?
(las celebraciones de los indigenas)

F   2. _____ ¿Qué veneraban los indígenas?
(las estrellas; la luna; el sol; la
naturaleza; el Gran Espítu)

F   3. _____ ¿Por qué daban fiestas los
indígenas?
(para rezarle al Gran Espíritu)

F   4. _____ ¿Cómo se preparaban para las
fiestas?
(se decoraban el cuerpo; se pintaban
la cara; se vestían en sus mejores
ropas)

F   5. _____ ¿Qué hacía el curandero durante las
celebraciones?
(guiaba la fiesta)

F   6. _____ ¿Qué hacían en las fiestas?
(bailaban; comían; se decoraban;
rezaban)

F   7. _____ En las celebraciones, ¿qué pedían
los indígenas cuando rezaban?
(una señal del Gran Espíritu)

I   8. _____ ¿Qué señal crees que los indígenas
esperaban?
(cualquier respuesta lógica)

E   9. _____ ¿Por qué crees que los indígenas
veneraban la naturaleza?
(cualquier respuesta lógica)

V   10. _____ ¿Qué significa la palabra *revelar*?
(decir; informar; cualquier respuesta
lógica)

☐ Questions Missed

Comprehension Scoring Guide	
Questions Missed	Level
0–1	Independent
1½–2	Ind./Inst.
2½	Instructional
3–4½	Inst./Frust.
5 +	Frustration

Retelling
Excellent
Satisfactory
Unsatisfactory

From Jerry L. Johns and Mayra C. Daniel, *Spanish Reading Inventory: Pre-Primer through Grade Eight* (2nd ed.). Copyright © 2010 by Kendall Hunt Publishing Company (1-800-247-3458). May be reproduced for noncommercial educational purposes. Website: www.kendallhunt.com

Student Copy is on page 112.

B 8183 (Grade 8) Activating Background: Lee el título a ti mismo. Luego dime qué crees que va a pasar en el cuento.

Background: Low ├────────┼────────┤ High

Nuestro Medio Ambiente

		MISCUES						
	Substitution	Insertion	Omission	Reversal	Repetition	Self-Correction of Unacceptable Miscue	Meaning Change (Significant Miscue)	
Además de usar plantas y animales como	7							
alimentos, la piel de los animales se aprovecha	15							
para hacer zapatos, la madera de los árboles se	24							
usa para construir casas, las fibras de las plantas	33							
de algodón para hacer faldas y camisas, y la lana	43							
de las ovejas para telar hilo y tela para coser	53							
trajes y abrigos. Hasta las fibras sintéticas que	61							
son tan usadas en la industria provienen de	69							
materias naturales que hay en abundancia en	76							
nuestro medio ambiente.	79							
El que digamos que el ser humano y el medio	89							
ambiente son interdependientes es una pequeña	95							
parte de este tema. En este milenio podemos	103							
llegar más lejos de lo que antes era posible y	113							
cambiar el medio ambiente usando	118							
conocimientos científicos y la tecnología. El	124							
ágil cerebro del ser humano nos facilita el que	133							
indaguemos profundamente en lo que la	139							
naturaleza pone a nuestro alcance.	144							
TOTAL								

Word Recognition Scoring Guide		
Total Miscues	Level	Significant Miscues
0–2	Independent	0–1
3–6	Ind./Inst.	2–3
7	Instructional	4
8–14	Inst./Frust.	5–6
15 +	Frustration	7 +

Total Miscues [ ]   **Significant Miscues** [ ]

Oral Reading Rate	Norm Group Percentile
___ WPM)8640	☐ 90 ☐ 75 ☐ 50 ☐ 25 ☐ 10

B 8183 (Grade 8)
Comprehension Questions

<table>
<tr><td></td><td></td><td></td><td>Retelling/Notes</td></tr>
</table>

T   1. _____ ¿De qué se tratan estos párrafos?
(del medio ambiente; de la
Interdependencia entre el ser humano
y el medio ambiente)

F   2. _____ ¿Qué utiliza el ser humano para
cambiar el medio ambiente?
(la ciencia; la tecnología)

F   3. _____ ¿Por qué tiene el ser humano la
habilidad de investigar el medio
ambiente?
(porque tiene un cerebro ágil)

F   4. _____ ¿De qué se hacen las fibras sintéticas?
(de materias naturales)

F   5. _____ Nombra algunos productos del medio
ambiente que el ser humano usa.
(las plantas; los animales; la madera;
el algodón; la lana [cualquier dos
respuestas])

F   6. _____ Según estos párrafos, ¿qué usa la
gente para hacer faldas y camisas?
(las fibras de las plantas de algodón)

F   7. _____ Según estos párrafos, ¿para qué se usa
la piel de los animales?
(para hacer zapatos)

I   8. _____ Dame algunos ejemplos de cómo el
ser humano ha cambiado el medio
ambiente.
(cualquier respuesta lógica)

E   9. _____ ¿Crees que es buena idea que el ser
humano cambie el medio ambiente?
(cualquier respuesta lógica)

V   10. _____ ¿Qué significa la palabra *fibras
sintéticas*?
(el material de algo; los hilos de la
tela; cualquier respuesta lógica)

☐ Questions Missed

Comprehension Scoring Guide	
Questions Missed	Level
0–1	Independent
1$\frac{1}{2}$–2	Ind./Inst.
2$\frac{1}{2}$	Instructional
3–4$\frac{1}{2}$	Inst./Frust.
5 +	Frustration

Retelling
Excellent
Satisfactory
Unsatisfactory

Miscue Totals and Reading Behavior Summary Charts

Directions: Record the number of miscues from all passages at the student's independent, instructional, and instructional/frustration levels. Total each category. Follow the same procedure for the other reading behaviors. Then make qualitative judgments about the student's reading and check the appropriate columns at the bottom of the cover page of the performance booklet.

Passages Read	Type of Miscue			
	Substitution	Insertion	Omission	Reversal
PP1				
PP2				
P				
1				
2				
3				
4				
5				
6				
7				
8				
TOTALS				

Passages Read	Other Reading Behaviors		
	Repetition	Self-Correction of Unacceptable Miscue	Meaning Change
PP1			
PP2			
P			
1			
2			
3			
4			
5			
6			
7			
8			
TOTALS			

Summary of Student's Comprehension Performance

	ANALYSIS BY TYPE OF QUESTION				
Grade	Fact Oral	Topic Oral	Evaluation Oral	Inference Oral	Vocabulary Oral
P	___/6	___/1	___/1	___/1	___/1
1	___/6	___/1	___/1	___/1	___/1
2	___/6	___/1	___/1	___/1	___/1
3	___/6	___/1	___/1	___/1	___/1
4	___/6	___/1	___/1	___/1	___/1
5	___/6	___/1	___/1	___/1	___/1
6	___/6	___/1	___/1	___/1	___/1
7	___/6	___/1	___/1	___/1	___/1
8	___/6	___/1	___/1	___/1	___/1
Ratio Missed	___/___	___/___	___/___	___/___	___/___
Percent Missed	___%	___%	___%	___%	___%

Class Summary Chart

Student	Date	Levels				Consistent Strengths (+) and/or Weaknesses (−)												
						Comprehension					Word Recognition							
		Independent	Instructional	Frustration	Listening	Fact	Topic	Inference	Evaluation	Vocabulary	Substitutions	Corrections	Repetitions	Omissions	Punctuation	Phonics	Context

Development of the Spanish Reading Inventory

Twenty-two passages from the Basic Reading Inventory (Johns, 2008) served as the basis for Form A and Form B of the Spanish Reading Inventory. After the passages were prepared, a number of speakers from different countries (Columbia, Cuba, El Salvador, Guatemala, Mexico, Nicaragua, Puerto Rico) and states (California, Florida, Illinois, Iowa, Texas, Washington,) provided input on passage content, specific word choices, and the comprehension questions. Once the passages were refined, two different readability formulas were applied to the passages as one way to estimate difficulty levels.

The FRASE readability formula was developed by Vari-Cartier (1981) from the well known and widely used Fry (1968) readability formula. FRASE means Fry Readability Adapted for Spanish Evaluation. This formula was validated by using Spanish language textbooks at the secondary level and is intended for "assessing the readability and difficulty of second language teaching materials" (Vari-Cartier, 1981, p. 147). The formula ratings of difficulty are based on descriptions: beginning level I, intermediate level II, advanced intermediate level III, and advanced level IV. There are no grade levels associated with these levels; nevertheless, applying the formula to the passages provided some indication how the passages progressed in difficulty.

More than 50 years ago, Spaulding (1956) proposed a readability formula for Spanish. It employed word usage based on a density calculation and sentence complexity as measured by average sentence length. The formula provides ratings such as first reader level, very easy, easy, moderately difficult, and so on. Like the FRASE readability formula, no specific grade levels are provided for readability calculations.

While Spaulding's formula may be appropriate for English-speaking adults learning Spanish, the list of words upon which the formula is based might cause a great deal of trouble for primary and middle grade students. There are words commonly used (e.g., *amarillo* and *pelota*) which fail to make Spaulding's word list. In calculating the Spaulding readability level, a judgment was made as to whether a particular word not on the list would contribute to the word density score when determining the level.

Both formulas were applied to the passages in the Spanish Reading Inventory. The readability ratings are presented in Table B.1. The levels obtained by applying the FRASE readability formula to the passages show a general progression from easy to more difficult. The levels from the Spaulding formula, with the exception of the first passage in Form A, increase in difficulty for the passages within each form.

Description and Rationale for Word List Development

A total of 400 elementary students read the word lists and passages. The word lists in Form A were read by 268 students (139 boys and 129 girls). In Form B, 132 students read the word lists

Table B.1

Readability Estimates for Passages in the Spanish Reading Inventory

	Readability Formula	
Form and Level	**Vari-Cartier FRASE**	**Spaulding**
AAA	Below Beginning Level I	Difficult
AA	Below Beginning Level I	Very Easy
A	Below Beginning Level I	Easy
A 7141	Below Beginning Level I	Easy
A 8224	Beginning Level I	Easy
A 3183	Beginning Level I	Easy
A 5414	Intermediate Level II	Easy
A 8589	Advanced Intermediate Level III	Difficult
A 6687	Advanced Intermediate Level III	Moderately Difficult
A 3717	Advanced Intermediate Level IV	Exceptionally Difficult
A 8183	Beyond Advanced Level IV	Difficult
BBB	Below Beginning Level I	First Primer
BB	Below Beginning Level I	First Primer
B	Below Beginning Level I	Very Easy
B 7141	Below Beginning Level I	Very Easy
B 8224	Beginning Level I	Easy
B 3183	Below Beginning Level I	Easy
B 5414	Beginning Level I	Easy
B 8589	Intermediate Level II	Easy
B 6687	Intermediate Level II	Moderately Difficult
B 3717	Advanced Intermediate Level III	Moderately Difficult
B 8183	Advanced Intermediate Level III	Exceptionally Difficult

(72 boys and 60 girls). No students were above grade six. Teachers, ESL teachers, and other support personnel from California, Florida, Illinois, Iowa, Texas, Washington, and Guatemala participated in the tryouts for both the word lists and passages.

Word lists were expanded and refined based on research conducted by Daniel (2006) in a bilingual school in Illinois. Her research was based on the professional literature related to how Spanish speakers learn to read (Azurdia, 1998; Carrasquillo, 1998; Escamilla, 1999; Freeman & Freeman, 1996; Pérez & Torres-Guzmán, 1992). It is important to note that researchers (August & Hakuta, 1997; Calderón, 2001) have suggested that the professional literature offers little to explain a student's acquisition of reading in Spanish. Daniel documented the literacy development of Spanish-English bilinguals during small-group reading instruction in levels through second grade in a bilingual school in Illinois. Observations of students' challenges when attempting to read books written in Spanish led her to the construction of charts of Spanish letters and syllables as acquired by readers in increasing order of difficulty. These findings influenced the development of the word lists. Also used was a text by Costigan, Muñoz, Porter, and Quintana (1989) which includes word lists in Spanish, Scholastic's beginning literacy series (1998), and many *cartillas* (phonics-based materials) used in the past and the present in Spanish-speaking countries for initial literacy instruction. The use of *cartillas* does not suggest support for a one-sided approach to understanding and evaluating literacy development; however, *cartillas* were consulted because they offer a view of an instructional methodology that has been used to promote Spanish literacy for many years.

The word lists used in the first edition of the Spanish Reading Inventory (Johns, 1997) were modified based on Daniel's work (2006); however, the pre-primer and primer lists are largely unchanged from those used in the first edition of the inventory. The pre-primer word lists contain simple words with open syllables and include the first consonants frequently taught in Spanish reading: *m, p, s, t, l, n, d,* and *b.* One of the pre-primer word lists includes words with the letters *f, r,* the digraph *ch,* and three words of three syllables. Most of the three syllable words on the primer lists have open syllables. These include the following digraphs: *gu, ll, qu, ch,* and *rr.* The first-grade lists include some four syllable words and the following digraphs: *fl, gl, bl, pl, cl, br, dr, cr, gr, pr,* and *tr.*

Piloting of the lists indicated that some students in third grade were only able to read the second-grade list which suggests the list to be at the appropriate level to help evaluate students who may be struggling. The lists include four and five syllable words and words such as *enséñamelo, cómpramelo, tráigamela,* and *píntamelo* at the second-grade level which are the combination of command forms of the verbs *to show, to buy, to bring,* and *to paint* with a direct and an indirect object added at the end denoting *show it to me, buy it for me, bring it to me,* and *paint it for me.* These words were included at that level because although students may have heard these words in conversations, they are unlikely to have seen them in print. During the piloting of the lists, these words served to quite clearly differentiate students' decoding and comprehension levels. Most students in second grade could almost decode the words, but they struggled with how the placement of the accent gave the word its meaning. What makes the lists unique is that they also include words that students at second- and third-grade level probably have never heard. These lists address the top level of decoding and not comprehension. In the field testing, as anticipated, many words in the third-grade lists were found to be unknown to the students in the primary grades. These words were retained because they will help to reveal the students' reading proficiency given the highly alphabetic nature of the Spanish language. When learning to read in Spanish, students are taught how to decode up to about the end of the second grade as they navigate through books and engage in meaning-making with texts. After second grade, reading difficulty is not as relative to decoding as it is to the reader's repertoire of vocabulary, the length of the sentence being read, and the comprehension demands regulated by syntactic and semantic considerations. Some examples of words included that the primary students were not expected to know and indeed were found to be unfamiliar to most of the subjects in the piloting were *magnánimo, monocotiledóneo, polinización, escabullirse,* and *pentágono.* These are difficult words for any Spanish reader to decipher and therefore serve to identify the reader who is able to decode as compared to the one who comprehends. After the piloting, some words were moved to a different position in the words lists. The more difficult words were placed near the end of the lists to help prevent initial student frustration when beginning to read a list. Other words that proved to be difficult for the students to decode were those with the oral accented *u* and the *diéresis* accent (which in Spanish requires pronouncing the letter *u* in speech when the vowel is followed by another vowel). Some of the words with this feature, such as *pingüino* and *zarigüeya,* suggest these to be a challenge for students below second grade. It is quite possible that many students at this level have never seen the *ü* accented with the dieresis.

Many students in the field tests were able to pronounce even the words that were not part of their everyday lexicon; therefore, the words were assumed to be representative of the students' decoding ability. For example, Mariana, a second-grade student, successfully decoded all the words in the third-grade list until she stopped at the five-syllable word, *comprémostelo.* Although she could decode the syllables in the word, which is a combination of a possessive, a direct object pronoun, and an indirect object pronoun, she was unable to place the accent at the correct syllable and therefore was challenged to grasp the meaning of the word. Her face showed a quizzical questioning look as she made efforts to read. This type of difficulty was evident in many of the students evaluated in the field tests. The students were able to read the word lists until reaching the level of reading proficiency that suggested the reading selections would be neither decodable nor comprehensible.

Reading Passages and Questions

Passages were modified to achieve accessibility for Spanish-speaking students from different nations. Such differences in words are subtle yet powerful. The passages incorporate input from highly educated bilingual individuals from Cuba, Mexico, Peru, Puerto Rico, and Venezuela living both outside and inside the United States. Revisions helped to ensure that the passages would be appropriate and have the potential to be understood by speakers of various Spanish dialects. Field testing conducted in Guatemala, a country where various languages other than Spanish are spoken, was very helpful in highlighting where modifications were needed to increase the comprehensibility of the passages for monolingual and bilingual speakers of Spanish. Input from teachers working with bilingual populations from different Spanish-speaking countries in the United States highlighted words that would improve the Spanish Reading Inventory because they would eliminate cultural mismatch. A change in selected passages was to include proper names that would be more familiar to students than those used in the first edition of the Spanish Reading Inventory. Although it is a recent phenomenon in many Latin American countries for children to be given names in English, none were used in the inventory because these anglicisms tend to be pronounced like Spanish words yet they are not decodable using the rules of Spanish linguistics.

Other changes made for this edition of the Spanish Reading Inventory contribute to the universality of the passages. For example, one of the second-grade passages originally included the number 500. This number was changed because none of the second-grade students evaluated knew this number. Another change was to include the word *jets* because during pilot testing it became evident that this was the word used by students rather than the term *aviones de propulsión a chorro*. Similarly, the term *miles* was used because speakers of Spanish who live in the United States have adopted the use of the word *miles* while the metric system and the words *meter* and *kilometers* are used in Latin America and Spain. The choice of a selection about snow might be questioned since many Spanish speakers live in countries where it never snows; nevertheless, the selection remains in the inventory. Although some of the learners have not seen snow, the passage posed no special comprehension challenges in the field testing.

Partial field testing was conducted in a private English-Spanish bilingual program in Guatemala City, Guatemala, and in a Midwestern elementary school in Illinois. Word choice was further supported by an important difference noted in the field testing with students enrolled in transitional bilingual programs in the United States (educational programs that have the goal of English acquisition and transitioning students to the all-English classroom as expeditiously as possible rather than to promote biliteracy development). Across all age groups, the Guatemalan students evidenced more extensive lexicons. They consistently demonstrated their comprehension of the reading passages by answering questions using words that were not part of the passages to a much greater extent than students in the United States.

The regularity of Spanish often permits students to pronounce words; however, this ability does not necessarily translate into understanding the passages. For example, Alejandra was not able to understand the primer passage even though her scores in the word lists were strong through the first grade. Be cautious when you use the Spanish Reading Inventory and do not assume that the ability to pronounce words will transfer into the ability to read and comprehend the passages. One of the teachers who assisted with the field testing shared this observation:

When I administered the tests, I found that most of the students were able to slowly read the words on the vocabulary lists. Their ability to comprehend what they were reading, however, was for the most part, below the level initially indicated by the vocabulary [word list] component of the test. You may be happy to know that when I shared the results of the inventory with the students' teachers, they were in complete agreement with the performance levels indicated by it.

Keep in mind that the Spanish Reading Inventory is an informal test. Used with your observations and professional judgment, the Spanish Reading Inventory can help assess and estimate a student's ability to read Spanish.

References

Adams, M.J. (1990). *Beginning to read: Thinking and learning about print.* (A summary prepared by S.A. Stahl, J. Osborn, & F. Lehr). Champaign, IL: University of Illinois.

Allington, R.L. (2009). *What really matters in fluency: Research-based practices across the curriculum.* Boston: Pearson.

Allington, R.L. (2005). The other five *pillars* of effective reading instruction. *Reading Today, 22,* 3.

Allington, R.L., & McGill-Franzen, A. (1980). Word identification errors in isolation and in context: Apples vs. oranges. *The Reading Teacher, 33,* 795–800.

Anderson, B., & Joels, R.W. (1986). Informal reading inventories. *Reading Improvement, 23,* 299–302.

August, D., & Hakuta, K. (1997). *Improving schooling for language minority children: A research agenda.* Washington, DC: National Academy Press.

Azurdia, E. (1998). Integrando la fonética en el proceso de la lectura en español. In A. Carrasquillo & P. Segan (Eds.), *The teaching of reading in Spanish to the bilingual student* (pp. 87–100). Mahwah, NJ: Erlbaum.

Bass, J.F., Dasinger, S., Elish-Piper, L., Matthews, M.W., & Risko, V.J. (2008). *A declaration of reader's rights: Renewing our commitment to students.* Boston: Allyn and Bacon.

Berliner, D.C. (1981). Academic learning time and reading achievement. In J.T. Guthrie (Ed.), *Comprehension and teaching: Research reviews* (pp. 203–226). Newark, DE: International Reading Association.

Betts, E.A. (1946). *Foundations of reading instruction.* New York: American Book Company.

Calderón, M. (2001). Curricula and methodologies used to teach Spanish-speaking limited English proficient students to read English. In R.E. Slavin & M. Calderón (Eds.), *Effective programs for Latino students* (pp. 251–305). Mahwah, NJ: Erlbaum.

Carnine, D.W., Silbert, J., Kame'enui, E.J., & Tarver, S.G. (2004). *Direct instruction reading* (4th ed.). Upper Saddle River, NJ: Pearson.

Carrasquillo, A. (1998). Métodos más conocidos en la enseñanza de la lectura en español. In A. Carrasquillo & P. Segan (Eds.), *The teaching of reading in Spanish to the bilingual student* (pp. 101–123). Mahwah, NJ: Erlbaum.

Carver, R.P. (1989). Silent reading rates in grade equivalents. *Journal of Reading Behavior, 21,* 155–166.

Conrad, L.L., & Shanklin, N.L. (1999). Using miscues to understand students' reading. *Colorado Reading Council Journal, 10,* 21–32.

Cooter, R.B., & Perkins, J.H. (2007). Looking to the future with *The Reading Teacher*: 900-year-old sheep and papa na come! *The Reading Teacher, 61,* 4–7.

Cornejo, R. (1972). *Spanish high frequency word lists.* Austin, TX: Southwestern Educational Laboratory.

Costigan, S., Muñoz, C., Porter, M., & Quintana, J. (1989). *El sabelotodo: The bilingual teacher's best friend.* Carmel, CA: Hampton-Brown.

Daniel, M. (2006). *There are no schwas in Spanish.* Unpublished manuscript.

Ekwall, E.E. (1976). Informal reading inventories: The instructional level. *The Reading Teacher, 29,* 662–665.

Ekwall, E.E. (1974). Should repetitions be counted as errors? *The Reading Teacher, 27,* 365–367.

Elish-Piper, L., Johns, J.L., & Lenski, S.D. (2006). *Teaching reading pre-k—grade 3* (3rd ed.). Dubuque, IA: Kendall Hunt.

Enz, B. (1989). The 90% success solution. Paper presented at the International Reading Association annual convention, New Orleans.

Escamilla, K. (1999). Teaching literacy in Spanish. In R. De Villar & J. Tinajero (Eds.), *The power of two languages: Effective dual language use across the curriculum for academic success* (pp. 126–141). New York: MacMillan McGraw-Hill.

Felknor, C. (2000). Use of individual reading inventories with fourth-grade students on individual literacy plans. *Colorado Reading Council Journal, 11,* 15–17.

Felknor, C., Winterscheidt, V., & Benson, L. (1999). Thoughtful use of individual reading inventories. *Colorado Reading Council Journal, 10,* 10–20.

Fink, R. (2006). *Why Jane and John couldn't read—and how they learned: A new look at striving readers.* Newark, DE: International Reading Association.

Forman, J., & Sanders, M.E. (1998). *Project leap first grade norming study: 1993–1998.* Unpublished manuscript.

Freeman, D.E., & Freeman, Y.S. (1996). *Teaching reading in Spanish in the bilingual classroom.* Portsmouth, NH: Heinemann.

Fry, E.B. (1968). A readability formula that saves time. *Journal of Reading, 11,* 513–516, 575–578.

Gambrell, L.B., Wilson, R.M., & Gantt, W.N. (1981). Classroom observations of task-attending behaviors of good and poor readers. *Journal of Educational Research, 74,* 400–404.

Gilliam, B., Peña, S.C., & Mountain, L. (1980). The Fry graph applied to Spanish readability. *The Reading Teacher, 33,* 426–430.

Goodman, K.S. (1971). The search called reading. In H.M. Robinson (Ed.), *Coordinating reading instruction* (pp. 10–14). Glenview, IL: Scott, Foresman.

Goodman, Y.M., Watson, D.J., & Burke, C.L. (2005). *Reading miscue inventory: From evaluation to instruction* (2nd ed.). New York: Richard C. Owen.

Harris, A.J., & Sipay, E.R. (1990). *How to increase reading ability* (9th ed.). New York: Longman.

Harris, T.L., & Hodges, R.E. (Eds.) (1981). *A dictionary of reading and related terms.* Newark, DE: International Reading Association.

Harris, T.L., & Hodges, R.E. (Eds.) (1995). *The literacy dictionary: The vocabulary of reading and writing.* Newark, DE: International Reading Association.

Hasbrouck, J.E., & Tindal, G.A. (2006). Oral reading fluency norms: A valuable assessment tool for teachers. *The Reading Teacher, 59,* 636–644.

Hasbrouck, J.E., & Tindal, G. (1992). Curriculum-based oral reading fluency norms for students in grades 2 through 5. *Teaching Exceptional Children, 24,* 41–44.

Hays, W.S. (1975). Criteria for the instructional level of reading. Microfiche ED 117 665.

Homan, S.P., & Klesius, J.P. (1985). A re-examination of the IRI: Word recognition criteria. *Reading Horizons, 26,* 54–61.

International Reading Association. (2000). *Making a difference means making it different: A position statement of the International Reading Association.* Newark, DE: Author.

International Reading Association. (2007). *Teaching reading well: A synthesis of the International Reading Association's research on teacher preparation for reading instruction.* Newark, DE: Author.

Johns, J.L. (2008). *Basic Reading Inventory* (10th ed.). Dubuque, IA: Kendall Hunt.

Johns, J.L. (1990). Informal reading inventories: A holistic consideration of the instructional level. In N.D. Padak, T.V. Rasinski, & J. Logan (Eds.), *Twelfth yearbook of the College Reading Association* (pp. 135–140).

Johns, J.L. (1976). Informal reading inventories: A survey among professionals. *Illinois School Research and Development, 13,* 35–39.

Johns, J.L. (1997). Spanish reading inventory. Dubuque, IA: Kendall Hunt.

Johns, J.L., & Berglund, R.L. (2010). *Fluency: Differentiated interventions and progress-monitoring assessments* (4th ed.). Dubuque, IA: Kendall Hunt.

Johns, J.L., & Berglund, R.L. (2002). *Strategies for content area learning* (2nd ed.). Dubuque, IA: Kendall Hunt.

Johns, J.L., Berglund, R.L., & L'Allier (2007). *Fluency at a glance (flipchart)*. Dubuque, IA: Kendall Hunt.

Johns, J.L., & Lenski, S.D. (2010). *Improving reading: Interventions, strategies, and resources* (5th ed.). Dubuque, IA: Kendall Hunt.

Johns, J.L., Lenski, S.D., & Berglund, R.L. (2006). *Comprehension and vocabulary strategies for the elementary grades* (2nd ed.). Dubuque, IA: Kendall Hunt.

Johns, J.L., & Magliari, A.M. (1989). Informal reading inventories: Are the Betts criteria the best criteria? *Reading Improvement, 26,* 124–132.

Johnson, M.S., Kress, R.A., & Pikulski, J.J. (1987). *Informal reading inventories* (2nd ed.). Newark, DE: International Reading Association.

Jorgenson, G.W. (1977). Relationship of classroom behavior to the accuracy of the match between material difficulty and student ability. *Journal of Educational Psychology, 69,* 24–32.

Kibby, M.W. (1995). *Practical steps for informing literacy instruction: A diagnostic decision-making model.* Newark, DE: International Reading Association.

Lenski, S.D. (1998). *Schools that succeed on the IGAP reading test.* Bloomington, IL: Illinois Reading Council.

Lenski, S.D., Wham, M.A., Johns, J.L., & Caskey, M.M. (2006). *Reading and learning strategies: Middle grades through high school* (3rd ed.). Dubuque, IA: Kendall Hunt.

Leslie, L., & Caldwell, J. (1995). *Qualitative reading inventory—II.* New York: HarperCollins.

Lipson, M.Y., & Wixson, K.K. (2003). *Assessment and instruction of reading and writing difficulty: An interactive approach* (3rd ed.). Boston: Allyn and Bacon.

Manning, J.C. (1995). Ariston Metron. *The Reading Teacher, 48,* 650–659.

McCormick, S. (2003). *Instructing students who have literacy problems* (4th ed.). Upper Saddle River, NJ: Pearson.

McTague, B. (1997). Lessons from reading recovery for classroom teachers. *Illinois Reading Council Journal, 25,* 42–49.

Morris, J.A. (1990). A*n investigation of informal reading inventory scoring criteria with average second- and fourth-grade students.* Unpublished doctoral dissertation. DeKalb, IL: Northern Illinois University.

Morrow, L.M. (1988). Retelling stories as a diagnostic tool. In S.M. Glazer, L.W. Searfross, & L.M. Gentile (Eds.), *Re-examining reading diagnosis and instruction* (pp. 128–149). Newark, DE: International Reading Association.

National Reading Panel. (2000). *Teaching children to read: An evidence-based assessment of the scientific research literature on reading and its implications for reading instruction.* Washington, DC: National Institute of Child Health & Human Development.

O'Connor, R.E., Bell, K.M., Harty, K.R., Larkin, L.K., Sackor, S.M., & Zigmond, N. (2002). Teaching reading to poor readers in the intermediate grades: A comparison of text difficulty. *Journal of Educational Psychology, 94*(3), 474–485.

Pearson, P.D. (2007). An endangered species act for literary education. *Journal of Literary Research, 39(2),* 145–162.

Pérez, B., & Torres-Guzmán, M.E. (1992). *Learning in two worlds: An integrated Spanish/English approach.* New York: Longman.

Pikulski, J. (1974). A critical review: Informal reading inventories. *The Reading Teacher, 28,* 141–151.

Powell, W.R. (1970). Reappraising the criteria for interpreting informal inventories. In D.L. DeBoer (Ed.), *Reading diagnosis and evaluation* (pp. 100–109). Newark, DE: International Reading Association.

Prior, S.M., & Welling, K.A. (2001). Read in your head: A Vygotskian analysis of the transition from oral to silent reading. *Reading Psychology, 22,* 1–15.

Samuels, S.J. (2002). Reading fluency: Its development and assessment. In A.E. Farstrup & S.J. Samuels (Eds.), *What research has to say about reading instruction* (3rd ed.) (pp. 166–183). Newark, DE: International Reading Association.

Schell, L.M. (1982). The validity of the potential level via listening comprehension: A cautionary note. *Reading Psychology, 3,* 271–276.

Schell, L.M., & Hanna, G.S. (1981). Can informal reading inventories reveal strengths and weaknesses in comprehension subskills? *The Reading Teacher, 35,* 263–268.

Scholastic Inc. (1998). *Scholastic Cuentos Foneticos: Spanish version of Scholastic phonics readers.* New York: Scholastic Publishing Group.

Spache, G.D. (1976). *Diagnosing and correcting reading disabilities.* Boston: Allyn and Bacon.

Spaulding, S. (1956). A Spanish readability formula. *Modern Language Journal, 40,* 433–441.

Spiegel, D.L. (1995). A comparison of traditional remedial programs and reading recovery: Guidelines for success for all programs. *The Reading Teacher, 49,* 86–96.

Taylor, B.M., Pearson, P.D., Clark, K., & Walpole, S. (2002). Effective schools and accomplished teachers: Lessons about primary-grade reading instruction in low income schools. In B.M. Taylor & P.D. Pearson (Eds.), *Teaching reading: Effective schools, accomplished teachers* (pp. 3–72). Mahwah, NJ: Erlbaum.

Tierney, R.J. (1998). Literacy assessment reform: Shifting beliefs, principled possibilities, and emerging practices. *The Reading Teacher, 51,* 374–390.

Torgesen, J.K. (2004). Lessons learned from research on interventions for students who have difficulty learning to read. In P. McCardle & V. Chhabra (Eds.), *The voice of evidence in reading research* (pp. 355–382). Baltimore: Paul H. Brooks.

Valencia, S.W., & Buly, M.R. (2004). Behind test scores: What struggling readers *really* need. *The Reading Teacher, 57,* 520–531.

Vari-Carier, P. (1981). Development and validation of a new instrument to assess the readability of Spanish prose. *Modern Language Journal, 65,* 141–148.

Walpole, S., & McKenna, M.C. (2006). The role of informal reading inventories in assessing word recognition (Assessment column). *The Reading Teacher, 59,* 592–594.

Zeigler, L.L., & Johns, J.L. (2005). *Visualization: Using mental images to strengthen comprehension.* Dubuque, IA: Kendall Hunt.

Index